Planning and Equipping Educational Music Facilities

by Harold P. Geerdes

Contents

Preface

For many years, the Music Educators National Conference has recognized the importance of proper housing and good equipment for the efficient and effective teaching of music. This is the sixth publication of MENC devoted exclusively to this important subject. It is a revision and updating of the 1966 book, which (like its predecessors) was entitled *Music Buildings, Rooms and Equipment*. In 1932, the Music Education Research Council issued Bulletin No. 17, which was revised in 1938 and rewritten in 1949 and again in 1955. The 1966 edition received wide distribution and was used extensively during a period when many new music facilities were erected. Not all the music suites and auditoriums were equally successful. The need became apparent for a more extensive edition of the book with more attention to step-by-step planning procedures, technical aspects, and specialized requirements of music spaces. The present book is an attempt to meet that need.

The author wishes to acknowledge the use of material, in some cases extensive, from the 1966 edition. Alteration and expansion of this material was undertaken only when that seemed essential, and certain sections are retained much as they appeared in 1966. The present edition benefits from a close collaboration with R. Lawrence Kirkegaard, Manager of the Architectural Technologies Division of the Chicago office of Bolt Beranek & Newman, Inc., who carefully reviewed early drafts of the manuscript and who also developed with the author the soundsheet "Acoustics for the Music Educator" that accompanies this book. The recording, found inside the back cover, gives the reader an unusual opportunity to gain a clearer perception of acoustical subtleties by actually hearing musical examples in altered acoustical environments.

A major contribution was made by Russell Johnson and his firm, Russell Johnson Associates, New York City. His acoustical work on the Calvin College Fine Arts Center as a member of the Bolt Beranek & Newman firm was so successful that the author was motivated to spend a sabbatical year with them and to share the knowledge and background gained by writing this book. Mr. Johnson was consulted often, and his advice and review of various drafts of the manuscript proved to be invaluable, as were the drawings he provided here. The section on illumination and color found in Chapter 5 was updated by C. Harold Barcus, Professor of Architecture at Miami University, Oxford, Ohio, who also contributed this material to the 1966 edition.

Acknowledgement also is made to the following consultants for their assistance with various aspects of this publication: David Klepper, Klepper, Marshall, King Associates, Ltd., White Plains, New York. Gerald Marshall, Klepper, Marshall, King Associates, Ltd., White Plains, New York. Jerry L. Monson, The Wenger Corporation, Owatonna, Minnesota. Robert W. Wolff, Russell Johnson Associates, New York, New York. MENC is also grateful to all of the schools, colleges, and architects who submitted photographs and drawings, of which only a small portion could be included here.

Harold P. Geerdes

Chapter 1: Introduction

New approaches to education currently are reflected in changing concepts in the design of school buildings. These approaches have underscored the importance of providing specialized facilities to meet the needs of certain subjects, such as music. New technology and new materials in themselves have not proved to be panaceas for the space and equipment problems that beset many music teachers. However, the knowledge and experience accumulated through the school building boom of recent decades have clarified these needs and have made apparent the need to stress the special requirements of areas devoted to music teaching. The days of assigning the music class or ensemble to any available space are, thank goodness, long past.

The waste of time and energy, and the diminished productivity resulting from poor facilities, cannot be justified at a time when spiraling costs and increasing demands on the educational system place a high premium on effective teaching and accountability. Nor can adjusting or compromising a school music program to fit inadequate facilities be an acceptable approach today. To plan these facilities as though the schoolhouse exists in isolation from the community also is very short-sighted. Expanded adult education programs and increasing community use during nonschool hours make careful planning for such use imperative.

New buildings often have given music educators and school administrators a second chance. Unfortunately, many new facilities that do not work well for music also have been built. In the past, rather casual planning has been done mostly by an archi-

tect after briefing by the superintendent. This no longer is acceptable. A more viable approach involves team planning by the eventual users and the designers, with much interplay between them. Technical requirements for sound isolation, good room acoustics, and other functional capabilities are not left to chance, but are determined carefully by specialists working with a design team.

New approaches to teaching music may make new demands on traditional spaces. The acceptance of open schools places music teaching in an entirely different physical frame of reference. Electronic developments, with their varied implications for music education, must be accommodated. Wise and careful planning is needed to provide the optimum in equipment and the best possible facilities. Perhaps even more than in some other subject areas, the proper tools and a hospitable environment will do much to enrich the teaching of music.

Planning and Equipping Educational Music Facilities is intended to provide guidelines for the music educator, the administrator, the board of education, and the architect in designing and constructing new buildings or remodeling existing ones. While intended primarily for the elementary and secondary level, it is broad in scope, and it deals with music facilities at all levels through the university. It is concerned with the location, design, and size of the facilities; storage and auxiliary space provided; and equipment placed in those facilities. It also is concerned with auditoriums and music shells. In addition, it contains sample floor plans and photographs of recently completed facilities, a unique soundsheet demonstrating acoustical principles, as well as a bibliography of additional references. The specific purposes of this publication include the following:

1. To guide the thinking of the music educator with regard to the physical requirements that are necessary for the successful performance of his duties.

2. To further acquaint the administrator and architect with some of the specialized departmental needs with which they may be familiar only in general terms.

3. To suggest proven, satisfactory approaches to some of the problems that commonly arise in the design and construction of new music facilities.

4. To serve as a checklist of details to be considered in planning and furnishing the facilities so that the music instructor may be confident that his music room is properly located, contains adequate storage areas, has adequate room acoustics, is provided with good sound isolation, and is not encumbered by other serious flaws that could have been corrected if attended to in time.

5. To arm the music educator with facts and information he needs to substantiate his presentation to the administration and to the architect.

Planning and Equipping Educational Music Facilities can be used by the music educator in the following ways:

1. He may familiarize himself with this material before preliminary discussions are begun in order to be more knowledgeable and better able to discuss the problems intelligently.

2. If he wishes to study certain areas in greater depth, a bibliography of additional references is included. Many of these titles include references to other materials that also may be helpful to him.

3. He can make this publication available to the administrator, architect, board of education, and other responsible persons.

4. He may review pertinent sections of this publication as planning and construction progress.

5. He may use this material to evaluate existing facilities to see if departmental needs are being met as adequately as possible in the space available. He may gain ideas for remodeling or treating the present space to make it more adequate. He may be encouraged to accept his present facilities not as an inescapable handicap, but to seek ways to make them work better for the music program.

While this book contains a great deal of useful information, a word of caution is in order about its use. The cookbook approach with pat recipes to meet every need is dangerous if it is used as a substitute for experienced consultants in any of the special areas of a music building. Advances in technology, as well as improvements in music programs, have combined to make these experts more important that ever. Few educational architectural firms have such experts on their regular staffs, and they often must be brought in. To a greater or lesser degree, depending on its size and scope, every project needs their help. Engaging them is the best insurance the facility planner can have that the finished building will work as intended.

Chapter 2: Planning Music Facilities

Before effective planning can take place, there must be a general consensus regarding the community's basic educational philosophy and the nature and extent of the curriculum that arises from that philosophy. No single solution or set of solutions is ideal in every situation. A physical plant can successfully meet the needs of a community only when it is designed in terms of that community's particular educational philosophy and when it provides sufficient flexibility to accommodate reasonable modifications in that philosophy. The need for a strong, balanced music program must be demonstrated logically and con-

BILL ENGDAHL, HEDRICH-BLESSING

University of Iowa, Iowa City
Architects: Harrison & Abramovitz
The relationship of the school music program to that of the entire community should be explored.

vincingly by the music educator. When this is done, he will have far fewer difficulties in securing the facilities he needs to carry on that program.

The music educator must have an important voice in designing the music facilities. It is essential that he be consulted early in the planning stages and that his opinions be sought periodically thereafter. As the person who actually will be using the space and equipment provided, he is in a position to offer valuable practical advice. The school administration and architect have an obligation to consider seriously the suggestions that are contributed by all of the professional staff.

Music departments and music schools differ widely in the amount of attention they devote to each type of instruction—classes, private lessons, ensemble rehearsals, and so forth—and no architect can plan intelligently unless he is aware of the particular needs of his client. As a first step in planning, therefore, the instructional program must be outlined for the architect. As planning continues, the relationship of the school's music program to that of the entire community must be explored. After-hours use by community music agencies is increasingly common. Adult education offerings often include music. Extended use that keeps the music suite busy into the evening hours is meeting growing favor with educational facility planners. In some communities, it is only by establishing the needs of such full-time programs that new buildings can be sold to a constituency that stubbornly resists higher taxes. School bond issues are more likely to be approved when the taxpayers can envision the larger benefits that will accrue to them through the community center.

Just as the architect and administrator must be aware of the needs and problems of the music educator, the music educator must be aware of the needs and problems of the architect and administrator. The teacher need not hesitate to ask for the equipment and facilities that are necessary for the satisfactory performance of his duties. But he must be realistic in his requests, and he must be able to justify them in terms of the philosophy of the institution. Further, he must understand that the administration, which is subject to pressures from many sources, must reconcile the divergent interests of all parties, including the taxpayers.

The music educator and administrator share the responsibility for making certain that the facilities are adequate for the future needs of the school. Not only must increases in student and faculty personnel be anticipated, but contemplated changes in the nature or scope of the music curriculum also must be considered. It is important to provide for full use of numerous and sophisticated instructional media. These aids promise far greater efficiency and flexibility in teaching than was possible previously.

During the preliminary discussions, the music teacher should visit the music facilities of new schools nearby and talk with the teachers who have used the facilities to find out what features they like or dislike. Occasionally, there is some discrepancy between the theoretical usefulness of a feature and its actual value in the classroom. However, the teacher also should be concerned with the reasons for his colleagues' preferences, since some of those reasons may not be applicable to his own circumstances. Whenever possible, the concepts of multiuse and flexi-

bility should be explored and applied carefully. While compromises that would jeopardize the program must be avoided assiduously, there are many ways to maximize the use of facilities by careful planning. But "flexible" should not be construed to mean "compromise."

THE PLANNING COMMITTEE: A DESIGN TEAM

Even in these days of open schools and flexible space modules, music spaces tend to be inflexible and permanent. Planning, therefore, must be complete and accurate from the beginning. There is little, if any, chance to correct oversights or errors. The architect and administrator should add to the planning team an appropriate number of future users from both school and community. The team also should include consultants in special areas, such as acoustics, sound isolation, lighting, and auditorium design.

The planning team must be charged with real responsibilities and must take an active role with genuine involvement by all members. Its work must be given high priority, and a written record of all its deliberations should be kept. The team's recommendations must be written in a form that will serve as a basis for preliminary design sketches to be made by the architect. These sketches should be reviewed carefully by the team and made the subject of a written report to the administration. The complete team has an important role to play in the entire planning process, and their experience, expertise, and understanding of how each space is to be employed should be used as fully as possible.

PROCEDURES FOR PLANNING

No two projects are exactly alike, and a list of steps to be followed in planning cannot apply exactly to every situation. The following items may apply to the planning for a larger building of which the music area is only a part; or, if it is a separate facility, they can stand by themselves. In every case, each step is important and should not be left out. It is assumed that an architect has been retained and that the administration is about to put together a design team. They should:

1. Designate representatives of the school board or administration, music department, and other departments that may share in the use of common areas, such as the auditorium, to work with the architects and the consultants as a team.

2. Review the educational goals and the activities that will be carried on to achieve them; develop a program for the new facility; estimate space needs; establish a preliminary budget.

3. Proceed with the schematic design; review and refine it until it is satisfactory, at the same time getting cost estimates; incorporate the systems concepts (space design, sound system functions, and the like) that evolve out of the detailed information channeled from the user group; develop physical information, such as systems requiring conduit or other special provisions.

4. Proceed to the construction drawings with complete details—structural, mechanical, and electrical—including sound

and other electronic systems; determine the location of all fixed equipment and necessary wiring for same.

5. Make provision for detailed supervision of the actual construction so that all the special requirements, especially those relating to sound isolation, noise control, and acoustics, are adhered to strictly. Pay critical attention to airtight construction that will not permit sound to leak through to adjacent rooms.

6. Follow through and check out all spaces and the various systems and equipment; through performance testing, orient the user to take maximum advantage of the new facilities and equipment.

BUILDING CODES AND FIRE SAFETY REGULATIONS

Local and national building codes, as well as life safety guidelines and codes, play a strong part in the overall planning and detailed design of all buildings, but particularly those involving public places of assembly. It is the responsibility of the design team to research the applicable codes and comply with them. The restrictions they place are an additional challenge that the architect will have to meet.

HOW THE MUSIC TEACHER CAN HELP

The architect will appreciate the answers to several basic questions:

What are you going to do? The architect, like most laymen, does not know exactly what music educators want to do in their facilities. He may not even be sure of which questions are the right ones to ask. He needs to be told directly the nature of the teacher's intended activities, such as rehearsing a band, teaching a general music class, coaching an ensemble, instructing a beginning string class, showing a film, or giving a private lesson.

How many pupils are involved? In addition to the expected enrollment of each class or performing group for each teacher, the architect will need to know the anticipated growth for the next five to ten years. For some classes or organizations, he may want to know the maximum effective size of such a group.

How does this activity fit into the total school program? A good building is planned for the program it is to house. Thus, music teachers need to remember the need for a large assembly area where music organizations can be used to instruct the other students as well as the need for rehearsal rooms.[1] They also should remember that sharing music rooms with other classes may make it possible to build with better quality construction.

Experience has shown that planning done under the pressure of time is likely to be faulty, incomplete, or uneconomical. As much lead time as possible should be provided, so that faculty members' ideas can be reviewed and assimilated before they are presented to the architect. Because of the nature and variety of music learning experiences, proper planning must have acoustics and sound isolation in mind from the start. In the early stages of gathering ideas, it is essential to consider the implications for sound isolation and acoustics in each of the major

areas: classrooms, private studios, practice rooms, large rehearsal rooms, concert facilities, offices, theory and listening laboratories, libraries, and storage areas. At this stage, it probably is desirable to anticipate future needs rather liberally, in line with the institution's own projected enrollment figures.

The size of the school or community is not always an adequate indication of the size of the music department or of its facility requirements. Schools in some small communities or small collegiate institutions may employ a large music staff and may offer both an extensive and intensive music program. Other schools may employ only one music specialist to do both the vocal and instrumental teaching. The institution's basic philosophy has an important influence on the decisions made about music facilities. Once the nature of the program has been established, a primary factor in determining music department needs becomes the number of teachers employed by the school for music activities. This is a more significant number than school enrollment or area population.

If the new building is replacing an old one, the number and size of classrooms can be estimated by beginning with the existing facility. Allowances must be made for desirable changes if existing rooms are too small or too large and for needed additions. Projected changes in the department's program or method of operation, such as small lecture sections being replaced by a large section or a related arts course being added to the department's program, will need to be considered. Demands that may be made on the classrooms by departments other than music must not be overlooked.

When a new building is added to a system or a new program developed, existing institutions with comparable curricular offerings and enrollment should be visited in order to establish a base for making plans. In the interest of economy, it will be necessary to consider whether large ensemble rooms or the recital hall can be used as classrooms for part of the day, or whether teaching studios and small ensemble practice rooms also can serve small classes or seminars.

Just as it is necessary to answer questions about educational purposes before making decisions related to instructional areas, it also is important to inquire about traffic patterns as they will affect the function of auxiliary areas. This is especially important for planning band, choir, and orchestra rehearsal rooms. With the large numbers of students involved and the complex movement necessary to pick up music and an instrument and find a seat, smooth traffic flow helps guarantee orderly entry and a saving of time before the rehearsal actually can begin. Taking the preliminary sketches and following a typical student or two into and out of the different areas is helpful in assuring a good traffic pattern.

Asking questions such as the following also will be helpful:

1. Should the student pass through the instrument storage room to check out his instrument before each rehearsal?

2. Are rehearsal folios picked up and returned to the music library at each rehearsal?

3. Will students need to get their instruments or folios from storage areas while another rehearsal is in progress?

4. Are uniforms and equipment distributed to the student out of the storage rooms, or is the area used only for dead storage during the summer?

[1]Karl D. Ernst and Charles L. Gary, eds., *Music in General Education* (Washington: Music Educators National Conference, 1965), p. 10-11.

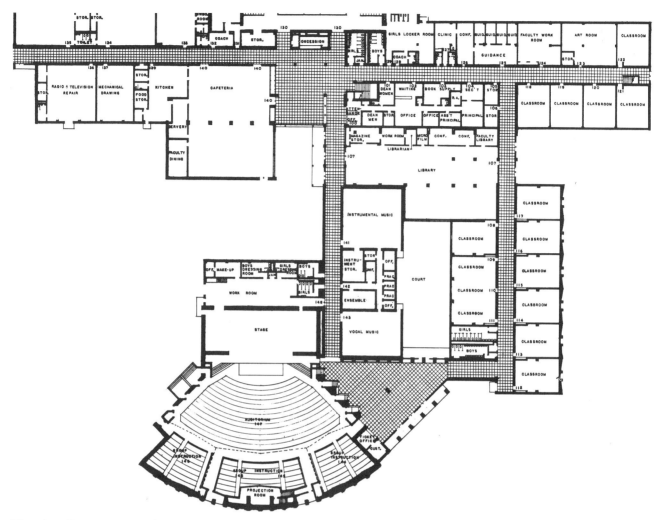

Theodore Roosevelt High School, Kent, Ohio
Architects: Dela Motte, Larson, Nassau & Associates
Music facilities should be located near the auditorium, with convenient access from the rest of the school.

5. Will there be drinking fountains? To avoid congestion, are they best placed inside or outside the rehearsal room?

Answers to these and similar questions will influence the planning of such auxiliary area details as relative locations, size, and number of doors.

LOCATION OF MUSIC FACILITIES

A major consideration in planning music facilities is the location of the rooms, offices, and rehearsal areas. Many factors are involved, including the relationship of the various music areas to each other as well as to other parts of the school and to the site. The building plans and photographs in this chapter illustrate many points worthy of attention.

Desirable Locations

The location of music facilities in relation to the rest of the school plant must be made with convenience of movement for students and equipment in mind. There are distinct advantages to having the instrumental rehearsal hall near and on the same level as the auditorium. However, insisting on locating everything adjacent to the auditorium can create serious isolation problems. Although a corridor or storage area between the rehearsal hall and the stage can help provide sound isolation, sound locks with double sets of doors and a vestibule between them as well as isolation joints in floors and walls may be required. Special attention must be given to avoid a common wall between rehearsal rooms and the performance areas. Second or third floor locations should be avoided for instrumental rehearsal rooms unless a service elevator is provided for the heavy instruments and equipment, and unless expensive sound isolation construction is specified. The music unit should have a direct outside entrance near the parking lot. A loading dock near the stage and music suite should be reached easily from either the street or driveways. An outside entrance to the drill field is a consideration where marching bands are involved. The music suite should comprise a compact unit, especially when only one teacher is responsible for supervising all of the activities.

Though convenience to the rest of the school is a factor, a certain degree of isolation may be desirable to avoid disturbing other classes or to allow use of the music unit at night when the rest of the building is locked. Separate music buildings provide some of the features but they sacrifice ease of travel to the rest of the school. Fine arts centers in campus-type schools have provided solutions in some situations.[2]

In the preliminary discussions with the architect, the music staff should express preferences regarding the location of various elements within the music department as well as the location of the music department in relation to the total school. They clearly should understand, however, that once the first line is drawn on a sheet of paper, certain commitments for sound isolation and acoustics already are implied that may influence the excellence of the facility much more than they realize. The counsel of a competent acoustical expert is invaluable, particularly at this early stage. One of the biggest problems in school planning today is the fact that many states do not pay for consultants, and school boards often are not prepared to pay their fees. As a result, if the consultant is hired at all, more often than not he is retained when the project is too far along for him to be of maximum service. Some architects are reluctant to add another person whose input must be considered in each planning decision, and they prefer to execute the project alone. But the employment as early in the project as possible of consultants experienced in planning school music facilities is an essential prerequisite to a really successful music building. Additionally, these experts have much to offer in planning ordinary classrooms, offices, and other spaces in the modern school building.

A good consultant frequently can save equipment costs while assuring maximum functional capability once the music staff's requests have been conveyed to the design team. It is the consultant's responsibility to help the architect to achieve these goals in the way that, in his professional judgment, seems best, taking into consideration such factors as the site, materials of construction, and budgeted funds.

Undesirable Locations

A stage built in conjunction with a gymnasium and used as a music room is most undesirable, both acoustically and aesthetically. Scheduling problems are certain to arise from such a compromise: a music rehearsal cannot be conducted during gym classes or basketball practice. *Curtains and room dividers in no way can provide sufficient barrier to sound for music purposes.* Multipurpose rooms of other types are not suitable for music use unless they are designed originally as music rooms with other activities carried on within them, and not the reverse, which is more common. If at all possible, separate facilities should be provided for dissimilar activities.

Basement locations are undesirable because of possible dampness (which could damage valuable instruments), poor lighting, and often inconvenient access. Even more important, the usual low ceilings make even minimal acoustic qualities unobtainable for all but practice room use. Furthermore, basement rooms often are near noisy mechanical equipment.

Outdoor Concert Sites

Schools and communities frequently plan for outdoor musical performance areas. One aspect of outdoor music performance that sometimes is overlooked is the need for a very quiet site. It is hopeless to try to perform music outdoors in a noisy part of the city. In some instances, of course, the sound can be amplified to override the high level of background noise from traffic, but this too easily can become a caricature, not a real performance. Successful outdoor concert facilities are always in quiet locations, and these are becoming increasingly hard to find.

BUILDING SECURITY, TRAFFIC, AND PARKING

Some basic decisions related to traffic control and building security must be made early in the planning stage. The need for tight security in the music area can become a preponderant consideration in the design, and it should be studied very carefully. Many potential problems can be thwarted by careful forethought. Will there be times in the evening or on weekends when only the music facilities of the building will be used? Will toilets be available? What schedule of keys for the building is desirable? It may be wise, for example, to place certain auxiliary areas (instrument storage, music library, repair room) on the same key as the instrumental rehearsal hall so that certain personnel can move freely with one key. Developing answers to certain questions related to the keying of the building can avoid annoying inconveniences or lack of proper security.

Careful planning also is needed with respect to parking. Although this area concerns not only the music department, there are certain aspects of the music program that may have special bearing on decisions related to parking. Typical of the questions for which the architect needs answers are the following:

1. Will music organizations perform away from school, and will their travel involve moving heavy equipment?

2. Will the department present evening programs in the recital hall or auditorium?

3. Will community groups use the music suite at night?

4. Will noise in the parking area create a sound problem for music study?

CONVERTING AND REMODELING

Schools sometimes are faced with the possiblity of converting existing buildings, such as old auditoriums, gymnasiums, or cafeterias, into music facilities. This seldom can be done successfully, and where it is necessary, it usually ends in compromise. It occasionally has been done successfully, but only in cases where a feasibility study by professionals has determined that the building is capable of being remodeled and what the right way is to do it.

When conversion does seem wise, large open spaces provide an opportunity to construct a shell within the load-bearing walls of the building. Auditoriums, gymnasiums, and some old libraries offer this possibility and permit the necessary room height. Whether or not a building should be converted must be examined carefully by an engineer, an architect, and an acoustical consultant, as few old buildings have sufficient foundations to bear the heavy wall construction needed for adequate sound

---

[2]See page 8 for a further discussion of combined facilities for the fine arts.

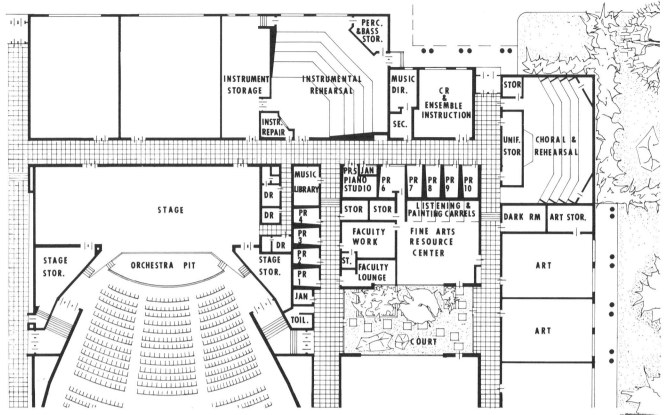

Northport (New York) Senior High School
Architects: Knappe & Johnson
Combined facilities for the fine arts usually contain areas for music, drama, visual arts, and sometimes dance.

isolation and the added weight of a heavy ceiling. In examining old facilities, internal traffic and external accessibility should not be overlooked. These admonitions are not intended to exclude the use of existing buildings for music purposes when the desired conditions can be met. It is necessary, however, to be certain that the desire for economy does not result in a facility entirely unsatisfactory for the music education process.

COMBINED FACILITIES FOR THE FINE ARTS

Many schools are establishing fine arts departments and housing art, drama, and music in units separate from the classroom area. Buildings of this nature usually consist of a music complex, a drama complex, and a visual arts complex. Dance sometimes may be included. The intricacy of these buildings requires the selection of an architect who has specialized in theatre construction, an acoustical consultant, and a theatre consultant to work with the architect from the initial planning through construction and completion. Only by this kind of team planning can a project be assured of quality construction and satisfactory results. References of interest in this area include "Better Architecture for the Performing Arts"[3] and *Theatre Design and Technology.*[4]

The drama complex may consist of a small theatre with a capacity of 300 to 500, work room, dressing areas, one or more classrooms, storage rooms, radio-television control and listening areas, costume storage and work area, and library. The art complex consists of classrooms, laboratories, offices, museums and display area, library, storage, offices, and facilities for security personnel. The size and extent of these units depends on the enrollment, community needs, and teacher orientation. In some areas of the country, fine arts departments are experiencing the most rapid growth in their history. In planning visual arts areas, one should not overlook photography laboratories, sculpture classrooms, shops for various crafts, and other forms of arts and crafts indigenous to local communities. Obviously, graphic arts teachers will be involved in planning, but music educators and administrators might find *Space and Facilities for Art Instruction*[5] helpful.

Another aspect of the music-drama-art-dance complex is that of combined festivals that frequently extend over several weeks of activity. These productions require highly specialized facilities that may result in total community effort. Seldom is there sufficient space provided for such musical extravaganzas as symphonic drama, dance-drama, ballet, and historical revues. Many of these need highly individualized and specialized facilities requiring architectural, acoustical, and engineering consultants who have given considerable time to research

[3]"Better Architecture for the Performing Arts," *Architectural Record*, Vol. 136 (December 1964), pp. 115-142.

[4]*Theatre Design and Technology. Journal of the U. S. Institute of Theatre Technology*, 245 West 52nd Street, New York, N. Y. 10019.

[5]U. S. Department of Health, Education and Welfare, *Space and Facilities for Art Instruction*, Special Publication No. 9 (Washington: U. S. Government Printing Office, 1963).

and study. In securing such consultants, the builders must thoroughly investigate the musical and dramatic background of those who are to advise on construction.

Special Uses of Fine Arts Facilities

In recent years, there has been a strong trend toward increased emphasis on education from the kindergarten through adulthood. Today, people of all ages are attending colleges and secondary schools—entire families are going to school, from the youngest in nursery classes to the parents in graduate seminars. This changing picture of education demands a more efficient use of buildings and facilities. In colleges, recital halls and auditoriums are used by students a high percentage of the day. In public schools, these same facilities are used for adult evening classes, conferences, lecture rooms, and other community functions. For economy and efficiency, schools should consider these eventualities in planning the fine arts facilities.

Undesirable Combinations

Schools in the past have been planned with various combination facilities that involved music rooms, supposedly in the interests of economy. These have included combinations of auditorium stage and music room, gymnasium-auditorium-music room, gymnasium-music room, and cafetorium. All of these must be viewed as undesirable. Few of the activities that would be carried on in such facilities have the same requirements. Unless the educational opportunities offered give the student the best learning situation, there are no savings. He must achieve the most for his efforts and learn to do his tasks in the best possible manner. Makeshift, made-do, unfortunate substitutions, undesirable combinations, and wrong tools are a poor approach toward education. Economies must not be made at the expense of the student; good planning by educators and professional architects should make such practices unnecessary. Although the roles that the administrator, music staff, and architect should play in an ideal collaboration have been explained above, the following checklists will guide each of these as they initiate their work:

BASIC PLANNING CONSIDERATIONS FOR THE ADMINISTRATOR

1. Have you developed a general philosophy of education for your institution?

2. Does your music staff understand this philosophy and their place in the overall program?

3. Have you determined the type of schedule the new building will carry and made certain that the music staff understands its implications for the music program?

4. Is your music staff actively involved in planning the new facilities?

5. Have you helped the music staff estimate the enrollments in the various activities planned in the music program?

6. Have you projected these enrollments for at least a five-year period in order to build for the future?

7. Have you and the music staff considered the implications of community involvement in music activities?

BASIC PLANNING CONSIDERATIONS FOR THE DIRECTOR OF MUSIC

1. Have you and the teachers involved in the new building developed a philosophy of music education?

2. Does this philosophy reflect the newest ideas in music education so that you will be building for the future?

3. Do those who will carry on the instruction fully understand their roles in the program of music education?

4. Have these teachers been given the opportunity to request facilities that will make it possible for them to do their best teaching?

5. Have you made the architect fully familiar with the type of program you want to carry on in the new building?

6. Have you studied your needs carefully and prepared yourself to resist being intimidated by the architect?

7. Are you coordinating your program with that of the drama department and others who may share the auditorium and its support spaces with you?

8. Have you given the architect your best estimates of the numbers of people involved in each phase of the music program?

9. Have you indicated to the architect any special requirements in acoustics, lighting, location, heating, humidity control, and so forth, that are necessary to your program?

10. Have you worked with the administrator to determine how the music activities will be scheduled in the new building?

11. Have you determined the equipment that will be needed to make the new facility functional?

12. Have you kept in mind possible changes in the music program in the future?

BASIC PLANNING CONSIDERATIONS FOR THE ARCHITECT

1. Have you visited other schools with a music program similar to that desired in the school you are to plan?

2. Have you met with the music staff to find out what they want to do in their teaching? Have you discussed the basic program and basic design with them and reviewed the schematics?

3. Have you visited classes and attended rehearsals and performances in the school so you are sensitive to their problems?

4. Are you familiar with, and have you sought assistance for, the special engineering and design problems of acoustics, sound transmission, lighting, auditorium seating and sightlines, stage rigging and lighting, traffic control, temperature and humidity control, and other special elements that are associated with music teaching and public performance?

5. Have you considered flexibility of facilities as the curriculum and teacher's role change and as community use of the facilities expands?

6. Are you prepared to suggest new ways that physical facilities can assist the music staff in reaching their objectives?

Music facilities can be divided into three general classifications depending on their function: those used for instructional activities, those serving in an auxiliary capacity, and those used for public performance. A typical music facility for a large school requires a wide variety of rooms and work areas. The needs of smaller schools probably are somewhat less but incorporate many of the same functional areas by telescoping or combining them into compact layouts.

INSTRUMENTAL REHEARSAL ROOMS

An instrumental rehearsal room must be large enough to accommodate the biggest band, orchestra, or combined group expected to use the facility, plus a vacant space of no less than six feet around the entire periphery of the room. Marching bands may place special space requirements on the room. Needs may vary from one size school to another, and from one section of the country to another, but 80 to 120 players is the normal range. In areas where the emphasis is on large bands, however, it is not unusual to find groups containing as many as 180 pupils. Orchestra space requirements are different from those for band, since string players require considerably more room. Also to be considered is the use of the room by community bands or orchestras. Combined use for both school and community groups may make it desirable to construct somewhat different

and probably larger rehearsal facilities with additional storage spaces.

Floor space is such an obvious requirement that much attention usually is given to it. The fact that sound levels produced by an instrumental ensemble literally can be deafening often is overlooked. This is particularly true if amplified instruments are used, as in rock bands. There are only two ways of reducing these levels to a degree where effective rehearsing is possible: (1) provide adequate volume (both floor area and ceiling height are critical), and (2) assure adequate areas and appropriate types and distribution of sound-absorbing materials on wall and ceiling surfaces.

Room Size

The floor area is largely determined by the number of students and whether they play wind or string instruments. An average figure of 25 to 35 square feet per student is desirable, while 20 to 30 square feet should be considered an absolute minimum, the upper limit being minimal for an orchestra. This will provide the necessary space for aisles, piano, music stands, and other equipment. The square footage per player allowed for a smaller ensemble should be somewhat more than for a large group, because circulation space requirements do not decrease proportionately. No student should sit against a wall or stand within 7½ feet of the ceiling. This is especially true of the bass horns and percussion instruments that usually are placed on the highest riser in the back of the ensemble.

Ceiling Height

The height of an instrumental rehearsal room also depends on the number of students involved, although the overall geometry of the room has an important bearing, too. A frequent mistake in rehearsal rooms is lack of sufficient ceiling height. Ceiling height must be planned for acoustic purposes. The effect of built-in or portable risers on this important parameter must not be overlooked. An average ceiling height of 22 to 30 feet is desirable. Heights of less than 18 feet should be considered only if sufficient floor space is provided to yield a volume in excess of 400 cubic feet per student. Anything less than a 14-foot ceiling in an instrumental rehearsal room should be questioned seriously. Even an 18-foot ceiling seldom produces a volume of 600 to 700 cubic feet per student, which studies have shown is required for loudness levels to approach comfortable limits.

Ceiling Reflective Surfaces

Regardless of volume and sound-absorption considerations, care must be taken to provide some appropriate overhead surfaces that reflect sound from one musician to another in order to maintain balance and ensemble. This is contrary to the general practice today of placing acoustical tile on the entire ceiling area in these rooms. Some ceiling reflection is essential to interplayer communication, especially if the volume of the room is large.

Risers

Differences of opinion will be found concerning the desirability of providing risers in instrumental rooms. Decided preference for flat floors has been demonstrated in new rooms built in the last decade or so, but architects currently are designing music rooms of both types according to the decision of those planning the facilities. If risers are desired, portable units that can be used or not seem to be the wisest option, since permanent risers built in concrete are inflexible and unchangeable, and they do not permit optimum use of the room by the marching band. Whichever is used—flat floors or built-in risers—the determination must be made early so that appropriate adjustments can be made in the other elements of the room design. If

JOSEPH MOLITOR

State University of New York, College at Cortland
Architects: Sargeant, Webster, Crenshaw & Folley
Adequate ceiling height is essential in instrumental rehearsal rooms.

Left: Macalester College, St. Paul, Minnesota
Lower left: Wausau (Wisconsin) West High School
Architects: John J. Flad & Associates
Appropriate ceiling reflective surfaces are necessary in both instrumental and choral rehearsal rooms.

Right: Plainwell (Michigan) Middle School
Architects: Daverman Associates
Ceiling height can be increased in ground floor rooms by excavating out below grade.

risers are built up from the grade level of the rest of the building, additional room height will be required. If the instrumental room is on the ground floor, additional ceiling height also can be achieved by excavating out below grade.

Floors

The relative merits of carpet, wood, or tile for rehearsal room floors still are being debated. The thin, easily maintained carpet usually found in school buildings has little acoustical value other than slightly reducing high frequency sound and quieting chair movement and foot scraping. The fact that performances seldom take place on carpeted floors could require an unnecessary adjustment on the part of musicians and conductors who have become accustomed to rehearsing on carpet. Many conductors feel that the vibrational response of wood floors provides a tactile condition that aids group ensemble. The only advantages of tile floors are cost and maintainability, and some studies have challenged even these. If the room is to be used for orches-

tra rehearsals or cello classes, some thought should be given to the effect of cello endpins on tile or wood flooring. Pieces of foot-square rubber-backed carpeting provide a convenient solution to this problem, and they easily can be carried in the music pocket of cello cases.

Acoustical Considerations

Room acoustics are discussed in detail in Chapter 4, but a few preliminary comments are in order here as precautions. A rehearsal room, unlike an auditorium, is a teaching space where such things as poor attacks, faulty intonation, and poor tone must be identified and corrected readily. A good rehearsal room will not duplicate (nor should it try to) the acoustics of a large performance hall, where the most desirable characteristics are balance, blend, and beauty of sound. Room proportion and shape are very critical and best left to the trained acoustician. All the sound-absorbing materials in an instrumental room should not be on one plane (ceiling only), as is so often seen, and some of it should be located in the height zone of the sound source. Extensive treatment of the walls also must be provided.

Ideally, bands and orchestras should not use the same rehearsal room. Recent research has indicated that for teaching

purposes, the band requires a much less reverberant space than does an orchestra. Also, the sound power level of a band can be considerably greater than that of an orchestra, and a larger room volume is required to keep the sound at a tolerable level for good teaching. Few schools, however, can afford the luxury of separate band and orchestra rooms. If scheduling permits, a room can be made to serve both functions satisfactorily by minor space compromises and by the introduction of relatively inexpensive variable acoustical elements. Bands have a predominance of sound energy concentrated in the lower frequencies, especially in the low brass instruments, that makes it very hard to avoid boominess in most band rooms. Orchestras, on the other hand, present less of this problem. Consequently, the room should be designed basically for band, with movable panels of appropriate materials that will help liven the room for full orchestra and string rehearsals.

Other Considerations

Heating and ventilating are discussed in detail in Chapter 5, but it should be mentioned here that year-round temperatures held at 68 to 74 degrees and humidity held at 40 to 50 percent by a very quiet air-handling system are essential in instrumen-

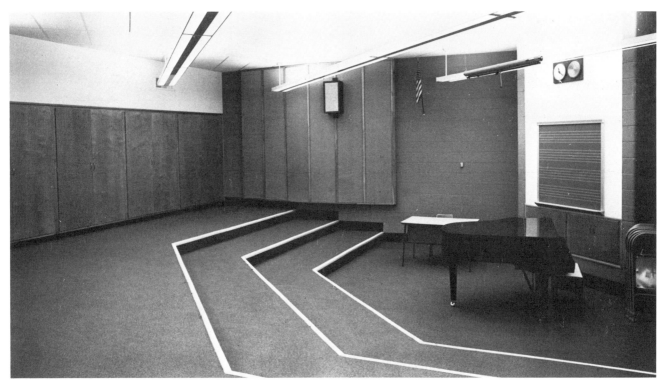

Norristown (Pennsylvania) Area High School
Architects: Anthony T. Rienzi & Associates
Permanent risers can be built into choral rehearsal rooms.

tal rooms, for the good of the instruments as much as for the comfort of the players. The instrumental rehearsal room probably will be used for instrumental classes and possibly even for theory or other music classes. Mounted chalkboards may be advisable, but acoustical considerations may require that their area be kept to a minimum or that they be covered by draperies or other adjustable absorption. Since rehearsal is the principal function of the room, no decision should be made that will detract from its ability to fulfill that role. For example, posture chairs with operable or detachable tablet arms should be purchased rather than using regular classroom seating.

Recording and Playback System

Provisions for tape recording and disc and tape playback systems should be included in room plans so that proper conduit can be installed at the time of construction. Provisions for closed-circuit television, movies, and slide projection also should be considered. Many rehearsal rooms currently incorporate microphone outlets with conduit and proper wiring that leads to a recording room. These use a talk-back system to provide two-way contact with the recording technician.

CHORAL REHEARSAL ROOMS

The specialized requirements of choral rehearsal rooms are somewhat different from those of facilities used exclusively for instrumental groups, except in terms of temperature, humidity, and acceptable noise levels. Space requirements are simplified, since it is not necessary to provide floor area for music stands

and instruments. Also, the high sound-power level of instrumental groups is not equalled by vocal ensembles.

Room Size

An area of at least 10 or 12 square feet is necessary for each singer if chairs are used on risers no less than 32 inches wide. If wide (36 or 40 inch) risers are preferred, extra space must be planned, with 15 to 18 or even 20 square feet per person not unusual. Reference to the catalogs of portable riser manufacturers will give many ideas of the space requirements for risers of different dimensions and for different types of room layouts.

Ceiling Height

Choral room ceilings do not have to be as high as those in instrumental rooms, but should be higher than regular classrooms and no less than 14 to 16 feet. Sufficient volume and enough ceiling height should be planned to provide a brighter and more reverberant acoustical environment in the choral room than in the instrumental room. Providing for acoustic adjustability with movable panels of sound absorbent materials will enhance the effectiveness and flexibility of the room.

Risers

Few, if any large, choral groups rehearse or perform without risers. The risers avoid obstructing the tone of singers in the back rows with the bodies of singers in front, and they also are essential for each observation of the conductor. An elevation of 6 to 10 inches and a width of 40 inches is adequate for permanent or semipermanent choral risers. Local building code and safety regulations enter into the choice of dimensions, too, and these will be the concern of the architect. As in the instrumental room, portable risers offer greater flexibility than permanent ones.

Other Considerations

Since piano accompaniment plays such an important role in the choir rehearsal, the room should provide adequate space for a grand piano. Some choir directors prefer to have their groups stand for at least part of the rehearsals as well as for concerts. In this case, providing enough flat floor space in front of the room to accommodate concert risers is a great aid. Seats in the choral room should ensure proper low-back support for the singers. Folding tablet armchairs will be useful for both classroom and rehearsal functions, since the room is likely to be used as a general classroom during nonchoral hours. Special fixed theatre-type seats with drop tablet arms may allow a width of only 36 inches between rows to be adequate. The use of the choral room for nonrehearsal functions suggests the inclusion of chalkboards, a projection screen, and closed-circuit television. Provision also should be made for a stereophonic (and perhaps quadraphonic) tape, disc, and cassette playback system; microphone outlets for recording and broadcasting should be considered.

COMBINED VOCAL-INSTRUMENTAL FACILITIES

Acoustically, one room cannot serve for both vocal and instrumental rehearsals with completely satisfactory results. Some communities, however, employ only one teacher and find it economically unsound to provide separate space for both instrumental and vocal groups. In fact, in many one-teacher situations, one room is the nucleus of all music activities. In the smallest music departments, a single, all-purpose room can be planned *in terms of space* to accommodate the vocal and instrumental group rehearsals, small ensembles, individual rehearsals, library, instrument and equipment storage, instrument repair facilities, office, and teaching studio, as well as various other music classes that may be scheduled. In terms of acoustics, however, few of these activities can be housed adequately in one room without creating undesirable conditions for the other activities. The best can be made of this situation if the room, because of the need to control the high sound level of a band, is designed to serve the band. Variable acoustical control will add very little to the cost of the room, and adjustable acoustic draperies or wall panels that can be retracted will help the room serve acceptably for choir and other needs. The room always

The Juilliard School, New York City
Architect: Pietro Belluschi
Associated Architects: Eduardo Catalano and Helge Westermann
Teaching studios should be available for private study by students.

will be a compromise, but it will be less so if this order of priorities is established. If such a combination room cannot be avoided, its eventual use for instrumental music alone can be kept foremost in its planning, with expansion to separate facilities as the ultimate goal.

TEACHING STUDIOS

Although group instruction is an important facet of the music program, ideal choral and instrumental programs supplement their group work with private study by their more talented and serious students. Some provision for this must be made in the building. The sound isolation and acoustical requirements for a good teaching studio are somewhat like those for practice rooms (see page 45). Because of frequent interruptions in the singing or playing for conversation, and because of the more concentrated effort expended in the private lesson, those criteria should be applied more stringently. Better sound isolation, more careful consideration of desirable acoustical ambience in studios used for different purposes (such as voice or brass instrument instruction), and more critical observance of noise criteria in the ventilating system all are needed in a good teaching studio. Here again, a competent acoustician should oversee the planning and construction.

A teaching studio requires more floor space than a practice room, although a room designed for ensemble practice may make an ideal teaching studio. An acceptable guideline for average studio size is 200 to 250 square feet. Some consideration should be given to the sound power levels of different performance media, and a pipe organ studio or percussion studio obviously will have different requirements from a voice or piano studio. Customizing teaching studios to suit individual teachers is possible through the use of portable sound-absorbing panels that are hung like pictures from a wall rail in sufficient quantity and in proper place to please the teacher. These may be included in the building design, or they can be fabricated inexpensively in a school shop.

At the college level, provision for one-to-one teaching becomes a matter of even greater concern. The number of studios, which usually double as faculty offices, corresponds directly to the number of applied music teachers. Unlike some other faculty offices, these cannot be shared. Although occupancy may be below the expected 50 to 60 hours per week, the college teacher must have his studio available for practicing and professional work at all times. If he commonly coaches chamber ensembles, such as string quartets or woodwind quintets, his office should be large enough to accommodate them, along with the desk, music files, and other paraphernalia he needs. Piano and voice faculty require room for grand pianos—a space that is desirable in every studio. Sound isolation considerations and interior acoustical treatment, which may include nonparallel walls and sound-absorbing wall panels, are not conducive to maximum use of wall area and floor space. Such individual requirements as chalkboards, mirrors, storage cabinets, and coat racks should be reviewed with the individual teacher, and every effort should be made to accommodate them so they can teach in their studio with maximum effectiveness.

PRACTICE ROOMS

Practice rooms are spaces peculiar to the teaching of music, and their design presents special problems not found in other elements of the school. Among these are isolation of sound, size and shape, ventilation, and provisions for supervision.

Number

The number of practice rooms needed by a music department should be related to the number of students involved and the school policy regarding practice room use. Some authorities recommend that students practice in school as much as possible so that assistance and supervision are available. Many feel that it is particularly important for those students who play the larger instruments to have practice facilities available because of the difficulty in carrying instruments home. The number of practice rooms needed may be arrived at by a survey-estimate of needed hours per school day. As a rule of thumb, a minimum of one practice room should be provided for each 40 students enrolled in the school's performance groups, or a maximum of one room for each 20 students in a more active program that stresses individual practice at school.

Location

The practice rooms should be convenient to the large rehearsal room in order to minimize moving heavy instruments and to maximize supervision. Efficient use of the rooms is possible, however, only if they are located and constructed in such a way that good isolation of their sound is achieved. Placing practice rooms along one wall of the rehearsal room is a very questionable practice, since neither the doors nor the glass that is desired for oversight can provide the required level of sound control, and the simultaneous use of both areas will be less than satisfactory. Practice rooms should be placed by themselves in a group, with library or storage rooms between them and the large rehearsal hall. Provision of a buffer zone between spaces where incompatible activities are to be carried on is the least expensive and best way to achieve good sound isolation. Special construction techniques are required in the walls, floors, ceilings, doors, and heating and ventilating systems. During construction, particular care must be taken to see that the rooms are literally airtight and thus soundtight. Masonry construction is advisable, with furred gypsum board or plaster skins applied to increase isolation. Gypsum board or plaster systems not employing masonry should be avoided scrupulously. This is true for rooms to be used for vocal as well as instrumental practice, because the piano, with its percussive attack and wide frequency range, is used in both and is one of the most difficult instruments to isolate. With the increasing use of amplified instruments in schools, proper location, careful design, and meticulous construction of practice rooms is more critical than ever, and an acoustical consultant experienced in such matters is essential.

Size and Shape

Practice rooms vary in size according to their function. Individual practice rooms of 55 to 65 square feet are quite satisfactory, although that size provides minimal extra space beyond that needed by an upright piano, a chair, and a music stand. With the need for ensemble and sectional rehearsals in the well-

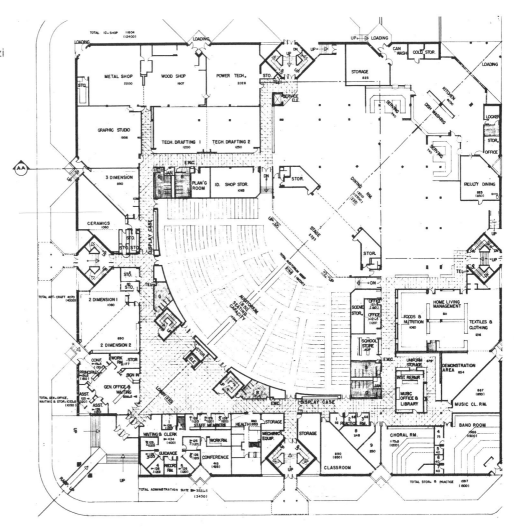

rounded music department, several larger practice rooms of 300 to 350 square feet should be included that can be shared by vocal and instrumental groups if necessary. These could accommodate grand pianos and perhaps even a small pipe organ. Parallel walls must be avoided within practice rooms unless compensated by considerable sound-absorbing treatment that is wide-range effective (at low, middle, and high frequencies). The important effect of size, shape, and wall and ceiling treatments on the acoustics of practice rooms is discussed in detail in Chapter 5.

Other Considerations

Air conditioning is becoming standard practice in schools throughout the country. This is not only an obvious improvement to the ventilation system in what often are cramped quarters, but there also are incidental assists to the effectiveness of sound isolation between rooms. Practice rooms can be arranged in blocks, spaced compactly, and even planned without outside windows. Temperature and humidity should be controlled to the same levels as in the classroom, with windows closed. Special attention must be paid to the duct layout and treatment of the air-handling system to prevent excessive fan noise and transfer of sound between rooms. Using the gentle sound of moving air to mask intruding sounds from neighboring rooms is a useful tool if it is implemented very carefully. In fact, some new music

buildings are including electronic noise generators for this very purpose, with a volume control so that the aspiring cellist can cover up the sound of the adjacent soprano with a pleasant purr. Construction to assure adequate sound isolation will make practice rooms more expensive than ordinary classrooms, but monetary cutbacks here are less justifiable than in any other part of the music suite.

Portable Practice Rooms

Portable practice rooms are an available option of rather recent development. Their most likely use is in remodeling projects, where an existing open room can be converted into very acceptable small practice rooms by the use of portable units. A small gymnasium, for example, can be converted into a bilevel practice suite through their use. Containing their own guaranteed sound isolation, acoustical treatment, lighting, and ventilation, these units are dependent only on the air-handling equipment of the space in which they stand and access to an electrical outlet. In either new or remodeling projects, they can provide a flexibility that permanent construction cannot achieve, while giving the appearance of regular built-in rooms. Size, shape, and height all are variable. Even more important, all critical isolation and acoustic criteria have been met, with the results guaranteed. If costs of construction are high, it may

Normandale Junior High School, Bloomington, Michigan
Portable practice rooms are especially useful in remodeling projects.

be less expensive to buy and install these portable units than to use conventional construction with adequate acoustical supervision. The consistency of their acoustical result is hard to match unless a very knowledgeable architect and contractor are both on the job.

MUSIC CLASSROOMS

Regular academic classrooms are used by many schools for classes in music history, appreciation, theory, composition, arranging, or other nonperformance subjects. If the teaching of these classes is to involve listening to music, these rooms are seldom completely satisfactory. For these uses, greater than ordinary care must be taken to block out extraneous sounds and to keep the noise level of the ventilating system below that normally allowed. The acoustics of the room also should provide for easy and pleasant listening, so a certain amount of liveness is desirable; acoustic tile should not be applied indiscriminately over the entire ceiling area.

A classroom that will be used primarily for general music classes needs ample storage space for books, records, rhythm in-

struments, Autoharps, piano keyboards, pictures, and similar equipment. Each such room should have a projection screen in a recessed ceiling pocket, with electric outlets in convenient places for easy use of projection equipment. If a classroom is to be used for theory classes, it is helpful to have staff lines painted on most of the chalkboards. However, this should not be done if music literature or appreciation classes will be the principal users of the room. Classrooms for college music education will need adequate locked shelf space or an adjacent storage room with shelves to accommodate large amounts of material. Campus-type schools and colleges also should consider supplying coathooks and shelf space in each classroom.

MUSIC TEACHING IN OPEN SCHOOLS

Music teachers are accustomed to having their own rooms and to teaching within four walls. Such conditions no longer are found in many new school buildings. The flexibility of schools with few fixed walls, and the effect of such design on the activi-

Broken Arrow Elementary
School, Lawrence, Kansas
Architects: The Shaver
Partnership
Music rooms can be
incorporated into open
space schools.

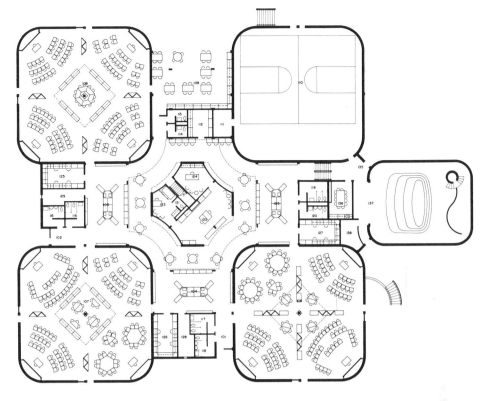

ties carried on within them, is one of the most significant educational developments of the twentieth century. Conventional approaches to the use of unconventional spaces do not always work. It is not within the scope of this book to discuss the philosophy or accomplishments of the open school. It can be helpful, however, to make a few general observations.

Any activity that involves formal lecture teaching is acceptable in the open room. As long as similar activities are going on in adjacent spaces, problems will be minimized as long as adequate distance exists. Such activities as playing instruments or listening to recordings over a conventional sound system will not be possible, since a high enough volume level for satisfactory listening would be above the general sound level of other activities in the large space. A zoned system, with many loudspeakers playing at low level, will work reasonably well only if very generous spaces exist between activities. Ideally, each student should be provided with a high-fidelity headset. An equipment unit housing cassette, tape, and disc playing facilities may feed into headphone outlets in the pupil area, perhaps in the carpeted floor for young children and in tabletops or carrels for older students. This system can offer a number of advantages, since it makes possible individualized instruction and use of self-teaching materials.[6] A useful idea recently developed involves a magnetic induction system that uses a wire loop placed under the carpeting or woven into it. Each student has a headset and can move freely about the room as he listens, unrestrained by wires and plugs.

Aside from these talking or listening activities, most music teaching requires performance, and this *must* be accommodated by special music rooms with the traditional four walls to confine the sound and to provide proper acoustics for effective rehearsal. Some educational facility planners may feel that music teachers are being unprogressive by insisting on such spaces, but just imagining the effects of a band rehearsal on all other teaching in an open space should settle the argument quickly.

CLASS PIANO ROOMS

Many school systems provide class instruction in piano as well as in band and orchestra instruments. The increasing availability of electronic keyboard instruments has made this practical even in smaller schools. A special room for this activity should be provided to accommodate either regular pianos or the electronic variety. Many piano teachers prefer the conventional piano because of its touch, sound, and complete 88-note keyboard. A room for such group instruction will impose many requirements in terms of sound isolation because the percussive action of the piano and the full range of its sound (both in frequency and in dynamics) make it one of the most difficult instruments to contain. Multiplying the number of pianos increases this problem. Careful consideration must be given to sound conditioning, with acoustical treatment of the walls and ceilings within the room and special insulation against transmitting sound to and from other adjacent music classrooms.

The room also will require chalkboards (both plain and with music staves), bulletin board space, music cabinet, and electrical outlets. Recording and playback facilities for television, disc, cassette, and tape should be provided, even if they are not initially included in the room's equipment.

Electronic keyboards are coming into increasing favor, and they offer many advantages that are hard to dispute. In spite of their limited range, different touch, and the electronic quality of their sound, new keyboards are much improved, and these criticisms are less valid today than they were just a few years ago. A survey of models now on the market will indicate instruments with expanded range, more typical piano touch, and acceptable sound. Great advantages are their lower cost, the possibility of using multiple-keyboard units that can be folded and rolled from one room to another, teacher-pupil contact through headsets that makes personalized instruction available even in the group situation, the possibility of playing records and tapes over the system, and the fact that almost any room can be used.

The ideal room for such use possesses certain amenities, such as carpeting on the floor plus some sound absorbent wall treatments. Careful planning of the room layout will enhance its efficient use. It is wise to choose the manufacturer and model in advance, since their dimensions vary. In-the-floor and in-the-wall cable runs will make it possible to avoid treacherous and unsightly wires on the floor for both the electrical and the electronic interconnections that are needed. Equipment manufacturers are pleased to help with details of advance planning, and teachers and administrators should not hesitate to take judicious advantage of their services.

LISTENING FACILITIES

As independent study becomes more common in high schools and open elementary classrooms, providing a listening center at

Norristown (Pennsylvania) Area High School
Architects: Anthony T. Rienzi & Associates
Multiple electronic keyboard units can be stored easily at the back of the room.

---

[6]This material is revised from the author's chapter, "The Environment for Learning," in *Individualized Instruction in Music*, compiled by Eunice Boardman Meske and Carroll Reinhart (Washington, D. C.: Music Educators National Conference, 1975).

Listening stations can be operated from a central position as shown, or designed for individual student use.

these levels becomes much more important than when this facility typically was found only at the college and university level. There are a number of approaches to the design and use of a listening center, and they are not mutually exclusive. These approaches are:

1. A number of soundproofed listening rooms or cubicles are provided, each with a tape, cassette, or record player. The student signs out material from a central location, such as the music department office or the resource center in the library, and is his own operator. This sytem exacts a considerable toll from the equipment and recordings, particularly phonodiscs.

2. A central position is provided for an operator who has a number of disc players, cassette decks, and tape players that can be channeled to any or all listening positions in this or an adjoining room. The student listens through headphones and does not handle source material. This system minimizes wear on records, tapes, and equipment, and the operator can double as a supervisor in the room. However, it does require special personnel to operate the listening facility.

3. A bank of tape players or cassettes is installed for individual student use with earphones, while the majority of listening stations are fed from a central control position. In this way, assignmemts that require stopping and replaying selected portions of a tape may be completed by the student himself without re-

course to the operator. These stations serve the autotutorial approach particularly well.

Designing a listening center is becoming a highly sophisticated and challenging job because of rapid changes in the field of storing and reproducing music. In 1975, two-channel stereophonic equipment is a must. Within a few years, four-channel quadraphonic equipment will be common in the home and very likely will be required in the schools. Although cassette players once were adequate only for recording speech, today's better tapes, improved equipment, and new low-noise and noise reducing electronics offer excellent capabilities for educational use. This can be done at a cost that makes it possible for every student to borrow from the school or have his own private cassette listening center. The savings in room, personnel, and electronics might better be met by having a cassette duplicator, provided there is no violation of copyright law. Whatever installation is made, it should be open-ended and designed for the most flexibility, so that unforeseen technical developments can be incorporated as they occur. Obsolescence is probably a greater threat here than in any other area of the music facility.

The equipment to be used, the number and kind of listening stations, and the desired atmosphere in the room all will have a bearing on its layout. Increasing favor has been shown in listening rooms that avoid the institutional look and that, by the use of tables, lamps, and comfortable furniture, seem more like lounges or living rooms. Attention should be given in advance to the special electrical needs for such a room. Ideally, the room should be quite dead acoustically, even though most if not all listening will be over headphones.

ELECTRONIC MUSIC STUDIOS

Will the new music facility provide space and equipment for the composition of electronic music? Today, every large university and many small ones have studios staffed by faculty members qualified and trained to work and teach in this booming field. Discussion of equipment needs for the electronic music studio is found in Chapter 5, page 60. Acoustically, the room should be very dead because of high monitoring levels and the need to avoid coloration of the sound by room effects. It also should be very well insulated from other music rooms.

AUXILIARY AREAS

Offices

For a music program to function smoothly, there must be a well-located director's office. Frequently, it is located adjacent to the teacher's rehearsal hall. Windows often are provided that enable the director to view rehearsals or practicing being done in the hall. This location places severe but not impossible requirements on the shared wall and the window between the two areas. If the need for a really quiet office seems paramount, it should be provided with a sound lock (a vestibule at the entrance with acoustical doors at each end) or located off an adjacent work area that could serve the same purpose. The office should not contain music library files, repair facilities, or other equipment that will produce a lot of student traffic and that better belongs elsewhere. If the office is to double as a teaching studio, it must be large enough to accommodate a piano, several chairs, and a tape recorder, as well as filing cabinets for correspondence and student records, and perhaps a cabinet for miscellaneous storage. In some situations, the director's office also may be called upon to double as a recording control room. In this case, the necessary conduit for audio cables to be concealed in the floor or wall, as well as extra electrical outlets, should be requested. Ideally, a separate room for recording will be provided, perhaps adjacent to the auditorium, but serving the rehearsal room as well (see page 60).

Not only the directors, but also music teachers who teach in several locations in a school (for example, harmony in a classroom, choir in the recital hall, general music in a specially equipped center) need an office to organize the many materials, instruments, and pieces of equipment with which they work. Offices also are essential for the department heads or the directors of performing groups because of the frequent contact they have with members of the community. The central offices of a college department or school of music reflect the organization and function of that particular department. If the offices provide only for administrative and secretarial staff, one size is indicated. If, in addition, the office area houses advisors, student records, and the like, a more complex unit is required. The

service area for the central office may range from one closet for supplies to a well-equipped room with several types of duplicating machines. It may include a check-out space for recordings and be adjacent to listening rooms; it also may provide a repository for the department's audiovisual equipment. If student inquiries are anticipated in large number, a counter may be planned in the office. This has the advantage of controlling office traffic to a large extent, separating the office personnel from the public and also providing space under the counter for storage.

Storage Areas

Adequate storage areas, planned with traffic patterns in mind, are important to the smooth functioning of a music facility. Storage with proper heat and humidity control is necessary for musical instruments, robes and uniforms, music scores, records, and various types of equipment. With careful planning, the storage areas can be placed conveniently and at the same time serve as buffers between two sound-producing areas, such as the instrumental and choral rehearsal halls.

Instrument Storage

Instrument storage facilities should be located so as to minimize the moving of instruments. Careful attention should be given to the patterns of movement through the room, with sufficient free floor space and ample distribution of compartments to avoid bottlenecks. Storage cabinets located within the rehearsal areas are inaccessible during rehearsal periods and frequently cause congestion during period changes. In some cases, this still might be the most advantageous location, in which case an extra 200 to 300 square feet of floor space should be allowed for them.

An instrument storage room should be at least 20 feet wide and 30 feet long. If there are windows, they should be placed high along one side. Glass block construction frequently is employed here. This type of window placement will permit the use of cabinets below the windows. Cabinets of various depths can be placed along two or three of the walls. The size of the cabinets usually should be no more than a maximum of 48 inches deep, 62 inches wide, and 83 inches high, including toe space. In some instances, it might be advantageous to extend cabinets to the ceiling, or to have a second set of cabinets built over the lower group for storage of equipment used only once or twice a year. A stepladder should be kept on hand for reaching this high shelving or locker space. Storage units can be built in by the building contractor or purchased separately. If prebuilt units are used, care must be taken to make sure that large units can pass through the door openings.

The instrument storage room should be well ventilated with a constant year-round temperature of 65 to 70 degrees Fahrenheit and a relative humidity of 35 to 50 percent, since many musical instruments are made of wood with glued joints. While some schools provide only shelves for storing instruments, this practice is undesirable. Most instruments have removable parts that easily are broken or jarred loose, and these may be lost or stolen if instruments are not kept in compartments. The instrument storage room should connect directly with the instrumental music room.

  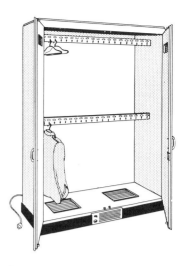

Closet dimensions should permit robes and uniforms to hang freely without touching the floor.

Instrument lockers made of wood or metal can be built to specifications for musical instrument storage and are available from manufacturers of storage equipment. If metal is used, carpeting should be affixed to the bottom of the cabinets to reduce noise and the possibility of damage, especially to large uncased brass instruments. Ventilation space should be provided in each locker door. The compartments should be large enough to avoid hitting door edges when removing instruments. Folding doors built to extend over several cabinet fronts are another method of protecting instruments. Lockers should be constructed to promote ready use as well as to protect the instruments. Deep lockers can be built into the wall area of surrounding corridors. The shelves and compartments may be designed to suit the instrument and equipment needs, or attractive and sturdy commercial cabinets purchased. In either case, a depth of 4 feet and a height of 6 feet would be adequate. Since most of the smaller musical instruments can be kept in regular student lockers, it may not be necessary to provide compartments for them. When these smaller instruments are not assigned to the students, such as during the summer, several instruments can be stored together in the large compartments.

Uniform and Robe Storage

Storage facilities should be planned for school-owned band and orchestra uniforms, choir robes, or vestments. This closet space should be cedar-lined. A well-constructed, close-fitting door will help protect against moths and dust. The closet space should be high enough so that uniforms and robes will not touch the floor when hanging on racks. Some provision should be made to space the uniforms and robes at equal intervals and to facilitate identification. A separate compartment for caps, belts, and other miscellaneous equipment also should be provided. Some directors require the band and choral uniforms to be left at school. Where this is done, provision should be made for dressing facilities located near the uniform storage area. For greater convenience, a set of folding racks on casters can be set up, loaded with uniforms, and rolled down the hall from the storage room to the dressing rooms. The dressing rooms should

be provided with bathing facilities, mirrors, and adequate dressing space. In some schools, these are rather elaborate facilities; in others, only minimum space is provided in the restrooms. One high school provides a uniform workroom equipped with sewing machines and personnel to alter and repair uniforms. Such a room also may be used as a workshop for making minor repairs on instruments. To facilitate distribution of equipment, a shelf on the lower half of a Dutch door is useful for the instrument and uniform storage rooms.

Music Library

Music libraries range from a single set of filing cabinets in the music room to the school of music library complete with stacks, reading rooms, charging desk, listening facilities, and work areas. In most colleges, there also are smaller libraries (band, orchestra, choral) that are more like the secondary school situations described here. Steel filing cabinets (full suspension with thumb locks) frequently are used for storing vocal and instrumental music. The letter-size file is satisfactory for choral music, whereas the legal-size file is desirable for most band and orchestra scores. Many schools use specially constructed cardboard boxes for music, allowing more wall space for storage. Box storage makes it possible to file new pieces in their proper places without shifting whole drawers of music to make space for the new purchases. Units also are available that store the music flat.

A sorting rack with five or six slanted shelves is valuable for distributing and arranging music for individual music folders; it also can serve as a folder cabinet. Many music directors prefer a specially constructed music folder cabinet that has individual compartments for each folio. This cabinet keeps the music orderly, facilitates distributing and collecting the music, makes possible a quick check of what music has been removed for individual practice, and also provides a convenient means of carrying music from the rehearsal area to concert stage. The partitions should have semicircular recesses so that folders can be grasped easily. Some directors prefer folio cabinets with larger, vertical slots, each of which will hold the three to six folders needed for each section. In this way, only one-fifth to one-third

Oberlin (Ohio) College Conservatory of Music
Architects: Minoru Yamasaki & Associates
Collegiate music departments may need to consider the desirability of a student lounge.

of the players need stop at the folio cabinet, and traffic flows more smoothly into and out of the room. The music library room should be separated from the instrument storage room. However, it usually is desirable and practical to have the two rooms adjoining, both opening off the music room, or stage, or both. Space in the library must be provided for work tables, supply cabinets, chairs, and a desk. In many smaller facilities, the music library equipment is kept in the office of the music director.

Instrument Repair Rooms

Some sort of facility should be provided for emergency instrument repairs. A special room is preferable, although many schools use a section of the music library or director's office for this purpose. Larger school systems have specially trained em-

ployees to take care of all instrument and equipment repairs. The minimum provision should be a workbench, stool, and a supply of appropriate tools.

Duplicating Rooms

Music departments usually have the facilities of the general office at their disposal, and they may not need copying or duplicating equipment in the music suite itself. Most collegiate departments or schools of music, and some school departments housed separately in a campus-type school, find a duplicating room invaluable. There are many times when the music department needs items copied—rehearsal schedules, instrumental parts of a student composition, football show routines, trip itineraries, vocalizes for the choir, songs in the public domain—and equipment should be readily available. The room should include enough counter space for several types of machines, an area for collating, and a sink.

ADDITIONAL FACILITIES

Because the music suite frequently is used at night when the remainder of the building is locked, some washrooms, toilet facilities, and custodial work areas must be provided within the music unit. In many instances, they are used as dressing rooms and must be convenient to the rest of the department. These facilities require about fifteen percent of the total floor space if adequate room is to be provided. If recitals to which the public is invited are given with the music unit, additional rest room space may be needed.

Collegiate music departments should consider the desirability of a lounge in which students can relax. If other study areas on the campus are some distance from the music facilities, one portion of the lounge might provide desk or table space.

Because of the heavy instruments and equipment that frequently must be moved in a music department, an elevator is desirable in a building of two or more floors. Also recommended is a loading dock adjacent to the parking area and as close to the auditorium stage as possible.

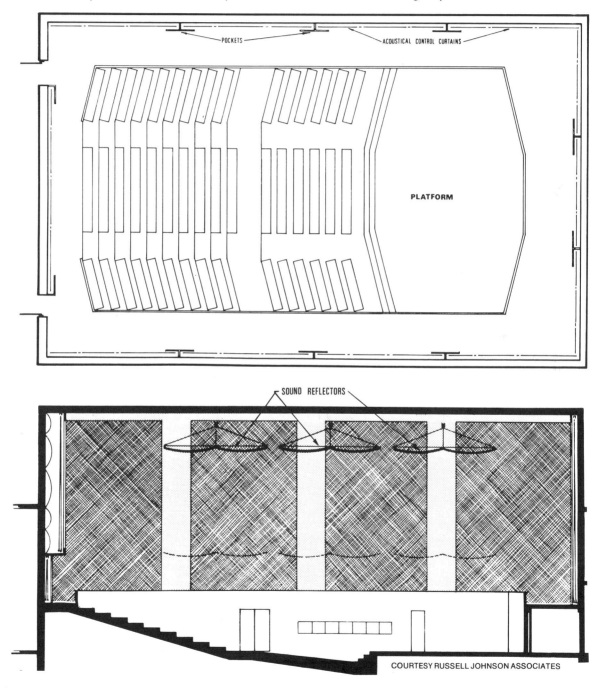

Floor plan and cross-section of a small recital hall for music only.

THE RECITAL HALL

A room intended for solo recitals, chamber music groups, or small ensembles may be termed a recital hall. Anything larger falls into the category of theatre or auditorium and is discussed later in this chapter. Planning the recital hall begins with a decision about the hall's intended use and its seating capacity. These will influence the size of its stage and bring about certain limitations of use. A hall seating 250 people cannot have a stage large enough to seat an orchestra and chorus, or even a large band. Such a small room would be uncomfortably loud with such powerful groups, even if space were available.

As with other large special-use rooms, one may think of a recital hall as also including several adjacent areas. Chief among these are performers' dressing rooms, provision for pipe-organ casework if the hall will have an organ, recording or broadcasting control room, storage rooms, warm-up areas, and a box office. In each case, the location of these and other special areas should be considered in relation to ease of concert operation. For example, a control room should have a view of the entire stage, and performers' rooms should be located on the same floor as the stage rather than a floor above or below; otherwise both lose much of their convenience.

Once the seating capacity of the recital hall has been determined, its shape, proportions, and the like become matters for the architect. A number of practical considerations, often overlooked even by experienced architects, are listed here. For example, a lighting dimmer control panel should be provided off-stage to dim audience lights during concerts. Separate circuits with wall switches, providing at least 30 footcandles of light, should be available for classroom use of the hall. A telephone system should connect the backstage area with the box office for efficiency in concert operation. Doors leading from corridors into the wings and from the wings onto the stage must be wide enough to provide for the passage of a grand piano—a small detail, yet one that often has been missed. If delivery of pianos or other large equipment is anticipated, the stage should have access to a loading dock. Even if the music building caters primarily to campus audiences, provision for parking areas should be considered.

Many recital halls double as a classroom or large lecture hall at certain times. Therefore, it may be necessary to provide theatre-type seats with folding tablet arms, so that the needs of both concert audiences and students may be met. A large ceiling-mounted projection screen can be useful, as well as connections to the recording studio. The projector should be located in a projection booth if at all possible.

COMBINED REHEARSAL-RECITAL FACILITIES

As a room for music performance, the recital hall is designed with strict criteria for sound isolation, adequate volume, sound treatment for proper acoustics, and a low level of ventilation noise. If well-designed, it automatically will include many of the requirements for an excellent rehearsal room. Combining recital and instrumental room functions is less satisfactory than combining recital and choral rooms. The requirements of a good choral room and a good small recital hall are so compatible that they easily can be combined into one room. The shallow stepped rows needed for seated choir lend themselves well to audience seating without a lot of waste space, which would not be true if the rows of seats were four feet apart as in a band or orchestra room. Fixed seating and a stage become essential to recital room functions, and a second lighting system that is dimmer-controlled will enhance the atmosphere and visual comfort at recitals. The stage easily can be made adequate for a choir on standing risers so they can do some of their rehearsing in concert formation. Three or four steps across the front of the entire stage down to the audience seating level can serve as permanent standing risers. The acoustics of a recital hall should be on the live side, which will favor choral singing. Recital halls need abundant volume to have excellent acoustics. The use of adjustable acoustical draperies on at least two walls not opposite each other makes the room suitable for varying types of performances.

THE AUDITORIUM

Basic Design Considerations

The most important school performance area is the large concert room or auditorium. Of all the disappointments that can accompany the move into new facilities, none is more saddening than an inadequate auditorium, for it is here that the music program meets the people and that all the intense effort and hard work should pay off. Unhappily, relatively few new auditoriums have met completely the objectives that seemed so obvious to the staff during the planning stage. It is staggering to consider the amount of money wasted when this happens. Even more appalling is the fact that for many years, students and community will be deprived of the joy and inspiration that come from performing in a fine hall; audiences will not receive the full benefits of performances; and the entire music program will be at a disadvantage. Planners, therefore, must approach the auditorium project with great care. Proper design will avoid facilities that are not suited to their particular needs, or that are designed for situations not appropriate to their communities. The auditorium should be designed first for educational use, and not for noneducational or commercial purposes.

Architects with experience in designing general facilities are not necessarily prepared to solve the problems associated with auditorium design. Those with experience in planning a movie theatre or a community multipurpose hall also may not be qualified. The wise and prudent planner will use every resource available to assure the success of his project, and this means securing specialists in acoustics, theatre planning, ventilating, and perhaps other related fields to supplement the architectural staff. Justifying the cost of these consultants can be difficult, since many states do not provide funds for their services. But they are essential to the success of any project so complicated as an auditorium. Educational auditoriums must serve many functions, usually carried out by amateurs. Design here is a particular challenge, since the special demands of amateurs often surpass those made by professionals.

The Audience-to-Stage Relationship

There are four basic auditorium and theatre designs, each of which puts the performers and the observers in a different relationship. A discussion of these four types and their implications for music performance follows.

Arena

The earliest theatre form was the arena, sometimes called central stage or theatre-in-the-round. This form places the audience fully around the stage on all sides. It is not suitable for school music performances, although there are a few concert halls of this type, such as the postwar Berlin Philharmonic Hall. Poor instrumental balance for listeners seated behind the band or orchestra, generally poor on-stage communication between players, and the loss of eye contact with many of the listeners are just three of the musical problems with this design.

Thrust Stage

The three-quarter-round thrust stage does not provide a hospitable environment for most music performances. With the audience surrounding the stage on three sides, many of the objections to the arena form apply here, including the impossibility of placing sound reflectors around the performers. A thrust stage also is unsatisfactory for music because of its dimensions. When properly designed for drama productions, it is no more than 20 feet wide and 25 feet deep, which will hardly accommodate the average band or orchestra. It may be suitable for chamber music and solo recital, but it creates problems for young and untrained speaking voices and therefore is not an ideal form for school playmakers either.

Proscenium Stage

The proscenium stage, sometimes called the "picture frame," has been a popular playhouse and concert hall form for several centuries. In it, the performers actually are in one room, and the audience is in another on the other side of the frame. The past seventy-five years of educational auditorium use in the United States have revealed many undesirable aspects of the large proscenium stage, particularly for music but also for many other common auditorium uses. A true proscenium must have a wide, tall stage house to be effective. This is necessary for acoustic coupling with the audience chamber, as well as for providing room for staging large-group performances and accommodating a stage rigging system. Not only is this large volume expensive, but it also places student musicians and actors out of scale where they are acoustically lost behind an arch that is 50 to 60 feet wide. Reducing the size of the arch visually with drapes or shutters is difficult and expensive, and it produces sightline problems unless the shape of the seating area also is changed. The typical proscenium is draped with heavy curtains and topped with a high stage house hung with sound-absorbing elements. Such a dead environment is hostile to music-making and demands a costly acoustical shell.

It is especially difficult to justify the wide arch, high stage house, and acoustical shell at a time when student-scaled non-

Stevens Point (Wisconsin)
  High School
Architects: John J. Flad
  & Associates
The proscenium stage
places the performers in
another room from the
audience.

The four basic theatre
designs each put the per-
formers and audience in a
different relationship.

COURTESY RUSSELL JOHNSON ASSOCIATES

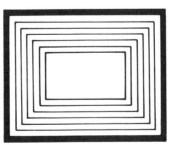

ARENA

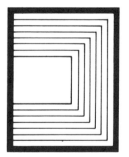

THRUST STAGE

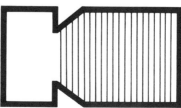

PROSCENIUM STAGE

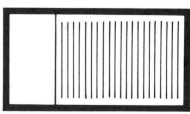

OPEN STAGE

mechanized multiform laboratory theatres of 75 to 150 seats are gaining favor among high school students and teachers.[7] Educational theatre groups rarely produce all their plays in a 900 to 1500 seat auditorium as they often were required to do in the past. If music ensembles must perform in a proscenium hall, some of the visual and acoustical problems can be avoided by placing instrumental and choral groups in front of the arch on large lifts that can serve as forestage for drama or as audience seating areas and orchestral pit when lowered to the appropriate levels. In this scheme, theatre settings can be put behind a movable sound-isolating wall and remain in place while concert rehearsals and performances take place in front. Unfortunately this solution, with its several motorized stage lifts, movable walls, and seat wagons, requires more funds than schools usually have to spend. However, it is far less costly than building two auditoriums. If it is not important to have daily change-over between concert and play rehearsals or performances, a forestage made of manually operable platforms can be designed for music performance. This may require removing several

rows of seats, individually or in sections, and could not be done frequently.

Open Stage

In the open stage, the audience and performers are in one room, with the stage at one end. It is the most successful design for dual use by music and theatre groups, and it is desirable for educational institutions where the auditorium must serve many different purposes. Most Western music was designed for similar rooms, and many of the world's finest concert halls use this format. Its advantages are many, including the considerable savings that result from the elimination of the costly stage house. More of the funds can be invested in the stage and its equipment, and a great deal of flexibility can be built in. The overall shape of the walls, ceiling, and floor easily can be designed so that a heavy stage shell for band or orchestra is not needed. Opera and musical theatre also can be set suitably in an open stage auditorium. The hard surfaces surrounding the stage help musicians hear each other and also reinforce speech. If space for shifting scenery is provided to the left and right of the stage, little or no flying equipment or fly space is required. Castered portable sound reflectors and, in some cases,

---

[7]This subject is covered extensively in Horace Robinson, *Architecture for the Educational Theatre* (Eugene: University of Oregon Press, 1971); and Richard Courtney, *The Drama Studio* (London: Pitman & Sons, 1963).

Alice Tully Hall, The Juilliard School, New York City
Architect: Pietro Belluschi
Associated Architects: Eduardo Catalano and Helge Westermann
The open stage places the audience and performer in the same room.

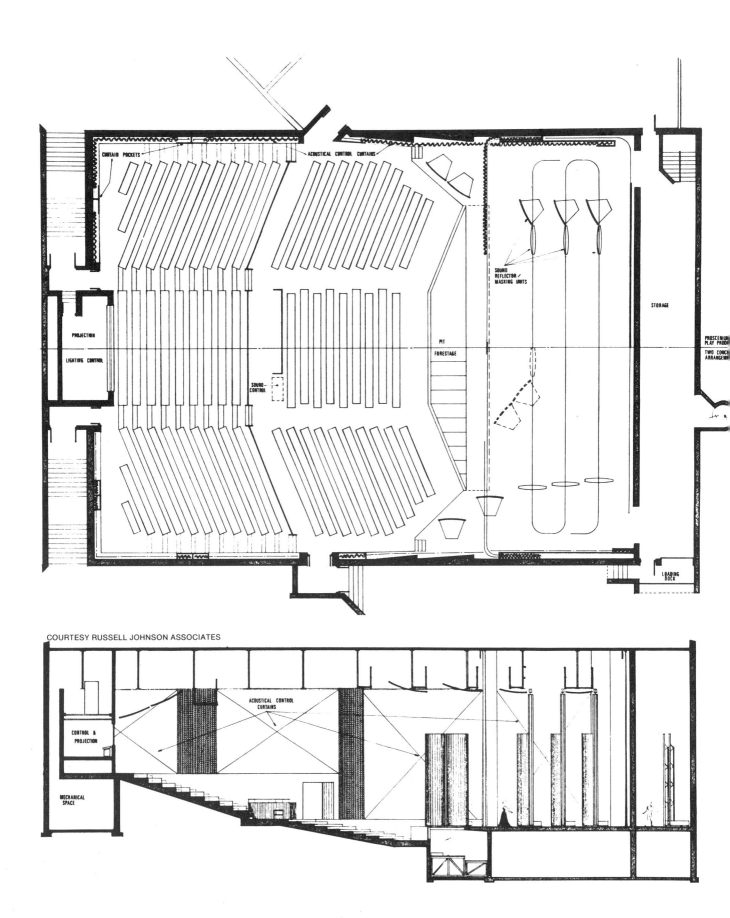

Floor plan and cross-section of an open stage auditorium.

fixed or pivoting panels, will make the stage completely flexible for use by large or small musical groups or for play production. Acoustical adjustment through the use of heavy curtains or banners on the side and rear walls help adapt the room for certain music and speech performances requiring lower reverberation times (see Chapter 5, pg. 47).

Scenic projection, both lens and direct beam, become important in the open stage. This can be either front or rear projection, but provision must be made early in the design for the method of choice. The rear wall (upstage) thus must be considered both for its visual function and as a stage reflector. A piece of fabric can be hung over this as an occasional backdrop. Anything is acceptable, so long as the exposed surface provides a suitable background for concerts as well as theatre. Catwalks provide access to lights and serve for temporary hanging of scenery. Curtain tracks provide for lateral movement of soft scenery. Pivoting sound reflective panels stage right and left work for both music and speech.

The playing size of the stage is determined by the sizes of the musical organizations, the stage requirements of musical or dramatic productions, and the scope of other activities proposed for this stage. An orchestra player should be allotted 18 square feet of floor space for himself, his instrument, and his music stand. This is a generally accepted figure for the minimum seating area, and it is much less than that recommended for the rehearsal hall because extra space at the front of the room is not needed here. A 100-piece orchestra requires about 1,800 square feet of floor space, or an area about 50 feet wide and 36 feet deep. The space requirements for band are about the same. The stage will have to be porportionately larger to accommodate combined choral and orchestral groups. The music educator must be certain to supply the architect with this kind of information.

Single or Multiple Use

One of the most important decisions is whether the space intended for music performance also will be used for drama activities. Space to be used only for concert events involves far fewer design compromises. However, performance areas for music alone should not be planned if no space exists elsewhere for play production. What sometimes happens in this instance is that lighting, rigging, scenery handling equipment, and other building elements necessary for drama are thrust into the planning process too late to be assimilated properly. This can leave the drama staff without facilities or with ones that provide an inhospitable environment. The result can be bad for music, too, as the late introduction of production elements, or adding them after construction is completed, usually hampers all activities. If a multiuse space is needed, it is better to establish this fact early and design accordingly.

School auditoriums seldom have been built with single-purpose use in mind. As schools consolidate, specialized facilities like the auditorium move toward serving the entire system or community. Forward-looking planners accept the broad concept of shared school and community use, particularly for libraries, gymnasiums, and auditoriums. Such an approach makes a multipurpose auditorium essential, and it must be designed for as much flexibility and adaptability as possible. The planning team should hold to a minimum any conflicts that arise between acoustical requirements and audience-performer relationships. The ideal solution, of course, is to have separate spaces for music and drama. A small theatre is a desirable supplement to the large auditorium, especially where enrollments and activities can support both facilities. Even small institutions should have a flexible room for theatrical experimentation and production in addition to the large auditorium. The need for this kind of space relates more to the creativity and activity of the drama department than to the size of the institution or the community.

Common Uses of the Auditorium

If the auditorium is to serve many fuctions, a list of common uses can be a helpful guide. The estimated frequency of each use also can be valuable to the planner. If compromises in design cannot be avoided, they should be made to favor the most frequent uses. A combined school/community auditorium might be used for the following:

1. Band, orchestra, and choir concerts
2. Solo recitals and chamber music programs
3. Musicals, operettas, or operas
4. Massed music festivals and concerts combining various groups
5. Popular folk or rock music
6. Ballet
7. Assemblies and lectures
8. Dramatic productions
9. Conferences and workshops
10. Movies and travelogues

Some of the presentations will be by students and others by visiting professionals. The latter will have some requirements not otherwise needed in a purely educational situation, such as special dressing rooms and possibly special stage and lighting needs.

Seating Capacity

The audience-performer relationship, room shape, and room size all have an effect on seating capacity, and the reverse is equally true. In actual practice, the audience area and stage must be designed together. Sightlines for the audience are tied to the height of the stage floor and the width of the stage. The location of masking devices for stage lighting and for off-stage areas depends on where the audience sits. The number of seats is interrelated with these and several other factors. In a commerical theatre and in certain other specific situations, it may be desirable to accommodate the entire potential attendance at one performance. In an educational situation, however, there are many cogent arguments for keeping the auditorium small. When a fine program is prepared, there may be value in having repeat performances. From this viewpoint, it might be practical to reduce the seating capacity of the auditorium or theatre and to spend the funds for better equipment so that the performances can be presented adequately.

A small hall enhances the interplay between performer and audience by making facial expressions and other nuances more perceptible. This is especially important for drama performances, where success tends to be in inverse proportion to the dis-

Calvin College, Grand Rapids, Michigan
Architects: Daverman Associates and The Perkins & Will Partnership
Acoustics: Russell Johnson
The open stage is adapted well to both drama and music performances.

tance of the audience from the stage. It is also helpful for choral concerts, chamber music programs, and solo recitals. From the acoustical aspect, seating capacity, which determines seating area, is so critical that once the size of the audience area is set, many of the acoustical parameters also are established. Each size auditorium has its own character and feeling. Some kinds of performances are optimized in halls of a certain size; others are compromised. Problems arise most frequently in halls that are too large or too small and that lack flexibility in form. The chart shown in Figure 1 summarizes the relationship between auditorium size and function and points to those combinations that yield the happiest results.

In trying to decide the size of a new auditorium, many planners have found it useful to make a study of actual audience size at events presented during the preceding year. An estimate of how many evenings a year the largest number of people would attend in the future is helpful in determining whether this justifies the high cost per seat of providing space for such an audience. This information, in addition to a careful review of future day-to-day needs is essential to intelligent planning. For a few really large productions a year, a gymnasium, field house, or community center may have to serve as best it can, leaving the smaller auditorium to serve in a more ideal way the many other events. Giving a concert to a standing-room-only audience in a smaller auditorium is certainly more satisfying than playing to a half-empty house in a huge hall. The educational goals of the orchestra, band, or choir are achieved as well if not better in such happy circumstances.

Continental Seating

One of the decisions to be made in considering how to accommodate the audience is whether the seats will be installed in unbroken rows with no rear-to-front aisles within the seating area, or in the more traditional method with two or three such aisles. In Europe, the former arrangement has been quite common; hence, the term "continental seating" is used to designate aisleless seating. The advantage of this type of seating is that the performer faces an unbroken audience area; where a center aisle once would have been, one now finds the best seats in the house. To permit convenient entry to the middle seats, the rows are placed far enough apart to permit patrons to sidle past occupied seats easily. More commodious seating arrangements result, without the arbitrary confinements of the code-regimented aisle seating arrangements. Rows are usually spaced 39 to 42 inches apart from back to back. Most new concert halls and opera houses in the United States and Canada, as well as a considerable number of school and college auditoriums, have adopted this seating system. Some halls have seats that push back a few inches to increase clearance, making a back-to-back dimension of 38 inches acceptable. Exit doors must be provided every five rows or every 25 feet along the side. Audience circulating patterns and lobby areas at the rear or sides are considerably different from those for conventional seating arrangements.

Conventional Seating

The traditional practice of back-to-front aisles still is desirable for many school auditoriums. Rows may be placed com-

		Figure 1. Ideal Auditorium Size for Various Presentations	
Seating Capacity	Performance Area	Most Successful Presentations	State Design and Audience Configuration
100 to 200	200 to 400 square feet	Recital, small ensemble, experimental drama, lecture, film	Flexible
300 to 500	350 to 600 square feet	Recital, chamber music, choir, drama, lecture, film	Flexible
600 to 1,000	600 to 1,000 square feet	All of the above, plus small orchestra and ballet (dance)	Open stage, semithrust, or modified proscenium; audience usually on one floor, but for 1,000 seats there may be one balcony
1,300 to 1,800	2,000 square feet plus side stages	Orchestra, band, choir, opera, ballet, drama, lyric theatre (drama with some sound reinforcement)	Open stage, semithrust, or modified proscenium; concert shell for music; one balcony
2,000 to 2,400	2,000 square feet plus side stages	All of those listed immediately above (drama and musical theatre require full sound reinforcement)	Open stage, modified proscenium, proscenium with concert shell; two balconies
2,500 to 3,000	over 2,000 square feet	Symphonic band (full sound system dependence for other events)	Open stage, modified proscenium, proscenium with concert shell; two to three balconies
over 3,000	over 2,500 square feet	Film, projected television, band, orchestra, choir (all performances require full sound system)	Proscenium stage, arenas, stadiums, etc.; two to three balconies; very long viewing distances

Krannert Playhouse,
   University of Illinois,
   Urbana
Architects: Harrison &
   Abramovitz
Continental seating allows
the performer to face an
unbroken audience area.

Krannert Great Hall,
   University of Illinois,
   Urbana
Architects: Harrison &
   Abramovitz
Conventional seating
includes several front-to-
back aisles in the audience
area.

fortably 36 to 37 inches apart from back to back; there is less possible friction between students, and access by the teacher to center seats is more convenient. The aisle space may offer an acoustical advantage if it provides enough hard, reflective area that is unobstructed even when the house if full. With fewer seats between aisles, there is apt to be less foot-trampling by latecomers. Conventional seating should be used in balconies, in halls more than 60 seats wide, and in halls with very steeply terraced seating areas.

Flexible Spaces for Seating

A caliper stage in a nonproscenium house can be adapted as a supplementary seating area for the audience. Chairs for this purpose should offer some of the amenities of regular audience seating, with padding and contours for comfort rather than posture. Seating should not get so close to the performers that they become uneasy. Precautions may be needed to assure safety if there is a sizable drop to the auditorium floor, and access aisles must be maintained.

Another flexible area for seating is the orchestra pit. If the pit is operable, the front should be made in removable sections so that, with pit floor at audience level, portable seating may be installed for special occasions. This seating can match the regular seats by being mounted on carts that lock into place, or they may, like the caliper chairs, be stacking or folding chairs. A pit for a fifty-piece orchestra with the railing removed can accommodate another one hundred audience members.

Other Seating Considerations

Options such as retractable seats, perforated seat bottoms, and aisle or under-seat carpeting must be chosen on the basis of the requirements and design concepts of the individual project. However, if the auditorium is to serve all its users well, these decisions must accede to acoustical considerations first of all.

Divisible Auditoriums

During the 1950's, planners were quick to recommend subdivisible auditorium configurations as a way to justify expenditure of tax money on classroom space rather than for seldom used auditoriums. Federal funding further served to encourage the divisibility concept; in fact, a number of quite good facilities were built and stand today as examples of what careful design and construction can produce. However, even the best of these facilities have been forced to live with compromises that would not have existed in nondivisible auditoriums. Subdivisibility is costly in terms of equipment and also in its waste of expensive building area. It adds unnecessary square footage within auditorium spaces (which always are built at premium cost) to provide for teaching positions that require otherwise unnecessary access space and that are less expensive elsewhere. The increased area degrades viewing conditions, substantially increases viewing distances, and results in impaired acoustics. Better facilities frequently can be built more efficiently and at lower cost if separated, with classrooms built as classrooms and auditoriums built as auditoriums. The considerably increased

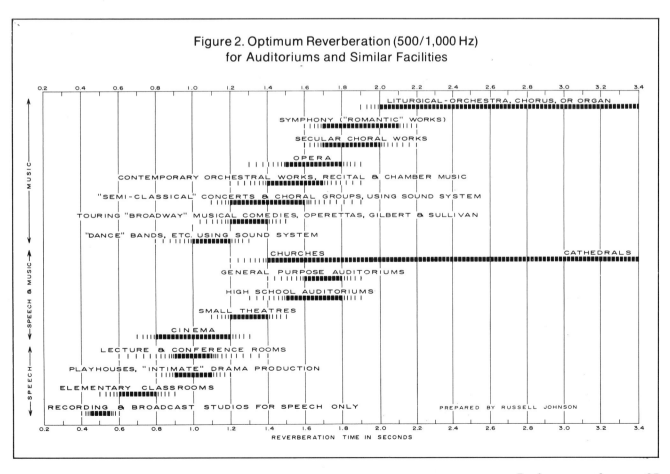

Figure 2. Optimum Reverberation (500/1,000 Hz) for Auditoriums and Similar Facilities

community use of the auditorium that invariably follows the opening of a new hall easily provides the price justification formerly sought by combining classrooms within the auditorium.

Acoustical Requirements

The optimum acoustical environments for the varied activities in an auditorium are not the same. While there are other acoustical factors to be considered, the most important is the reverberation time at middle frequencies, which is calculated according to an established formula. It requires instruments for actual accurate measurement, or it can be figured from blueprints in advance. Speech and drama require about 1 second, while music requires reverberation times of 1.5 to 2 seconds or more, depending on the space and the performance (see Figure 2). For speech, the listener wants most of the sound to arrive directly from the source, whereas for music, total envelopment by the sound is desirable. These conflicting requirements can be met by incorporating adjustable acoustical devices into the building. Without them, one or more of the uses must be compromised considerably.

THE STAGE

Doors

All doors entering on a stage must be of sufficient height and width to provide ready access to the stage. This is especially true of the scenery doors. They must be high enough to accommodate wide stage wagons, large instruments, and occasionally motor vehicles. The doors for scenery should be at least 8 feet wide and 14 feet tall, and all other doors leading to and from the stage should be extra-wide double doors. All exterior doors leading into the auditorium should be solid, have no windows that could allow light leaks, and be mounted so they do not rattle in the wind. All doors must operate silently. Panic bars on exit doors generally are required by law, but sometimes are rendered useless by padlocks and chains, which is an extremely dangerous practice. Doors should be gasketed to prevent a bypassing of the sound isolation construction, and threshold drop seals should be provided. Every attempt must be made to keep the sound of heavy rain or thunder from penetrating into the auditorium.

Apron and Calipers

Calipers provide interesting possibilities for antiphonal performance of music, overflow capabilities for large, massed groups on stage, and supplementary acting areas for the drama department. For concert use, the open floor area of the calipers enhances the acoustics somewhat. The stage apron should be wide enough that pianos and other equipment can be used in front of the main curtain. For certain musical performances, it may be advisable to extend the apron over the orchestra pit (see Chapter 4, p. 39).

The floor of the stage proper, if combined for music-theatre-dance use, should be white pine tongue-and-groove lumber with plywood subflooring laid on sleepers and resilient pads.

The floor should be stained a very dark brown—almost black—and one coat of nongloss sealer applied. Linoleum, hardboard, or other decks can be laid on this floor for special purposes. On both sides of the stage leading to the audience area, fixed or portable steps should be provided. The steps should be wide enough for musical instruments and other small properties to be carried from the auditorium to the stage, or to allow students to approach the stage two abreast.

Chairs and Risers

Chairs for the stage should be specified in sufficient quantity to be readily at hand for rehearsals and other stage uses. Stacking chairs stored on castered racks take a minimum of backstage room and yet are moved easily from storage into position for use.

Portable risers should be provided as part of regular stage equipment. For music performances, these include stepped risers for seated band, orchestra, or chorus, as well as a set of risers for the standing choir. Folding 4 x 6 foot platforms that have their own casters provide ease of movement and set-up and can be used for both music and dramatic performances. They are available in 8-inch heights, with increments of 8 inches up to 32 or 40 inches if desired. Storage space for risers and chairs convenient to the stage should not be overlooked. Hydraulically operated stage sections sometimes are included for drama use. However, these are very expensive and receive too little use in the typical school to justify their inclusion. Homemade risers, as compared to factory-built, present a safety and liability hazard that sould rule them out for school use. Manufacturers of such equipment have designed special hardware and carefully tested their products with a built-in safety factor that is hard to match.

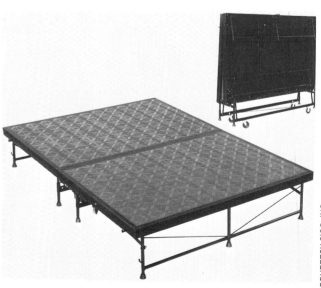

COURTESY SICO, INC.

Folding, castered platforms are easy to use and to store.

Lighting

There are many new concepts in stage lighting, whether the facility to be lighted is a proscenium theatre, open stage, or modified proscenium. The border and footlight installations once popular in school auditoriums no longer are considered adequate. In addition to sufficient downlights for concerts and other nontheatrical presentations, school auditoriums need stage lighting for a number of specific dramatic purposes. The amount of lighting and the types required depend on the design of the auditorium and the nature of the productions that are planned for it (see Chapter 6).

Front lighting from slots in the auditorium ceiling, serviced by catwalks, is highly desirable. Additional wall slots and a location for a follow spot in the rear of the auditorium are common. Spotlights are needed on battens, stands, or tormentor pipes to provide further illumination of the acting area. Borderlights and sometimes footlights are used for toning and blending. Beamlights are used for backlighting. Floodlights are used for background effects, and special footlights are needed for a cyclorama. Sidelighting sometimes is provided by spotlights from a mobile tower in the wings. An elaborate college or community theatre installation may include a light bridge. Open stages and modified proscenium stages frequently use projected backgrounds. The lamp house for scenic projection may be located on a catwalk above the stage area or in a ceiling slot above the front curtain.

The stage switchboard should be located at the rear of the auditorium in a lighting booth. In addition to operable windows and an intercom phone, monitor loud speakers also are needed so the operator can hear what is going on in the auditorium if the windows are closed during a performance. Switchboard facilities should service an adequate number of floor pockets, which will vary with the size of the auditorium, stage, and its lighting equipment. A dimmer system must be part of the lighting installations.

There never can be too many outlets. It is better to have many adequate outlets than to risk overloading a few. Normally, there should be three or four locations for floor pockets across both the right and left sides of the stage, across the back of the stage, and on each side of the acting area. Each pocket should be capable of handling three to six 3000-watt circuits. All wiring for stage lights must be kept off the floor. This sometimes is accomplished by using overhead flexible drops to service the ladders or towers. Tormenter lights are serviced from proscenium pockets. Auditorium and proscenium slots are serviced from standard stage pockets located within the slots.

University of Iowa, Iowa City
Architects: Harrison & Abramovitz
The stage switchboard should be located at the rear of the auditorium in a booth with operable windows and intercom phone.

Rigging

This book does not treat theatrical rigging systems or other drama-associated aspects of spaces shared by the two arts. On these matters, consultants should be called in. Other sources, listed in the bibliography, treat these subjects more completely than can be done here.

Cyclorama

It once was though that every school stage was adequately furnished if it had a cyclorama—a continuous curtain around the sides and rear of the stage. Since this curtain usually was made of heavy velour, its effect on stage acoustics when used for music was very detrimental. Every attempt should be made to avoid heavy draperies that make the stage dead and destroy the acoustical matching of the stage to the house. If absorbent curtains are used, they should retract into pockets. Withdrawing a cyclorama curtain into pockets is not practical unless the exposed rear stage wall presents an acceptable visual background for concerts and theatre. It should be made of wood, troweled block, brick, or concrete block. It should not be painted white or near-white, since light colored surfaces near performers make it difficult for them to see. If a surface pattern exists, the play director may want to use a cyclorama to cover the wall. This curtain, too, should not be too light in color. In some situations, castered sound reflecting panels and overhead-track supported pivoting panels can combine the functions of side masking curtains and concert shell side walls. These, along with fixed reflectors, are designed with the assistance of the acoustics and theatre consultants. Use of theatrical masking curtains, valences and cyclorama to mask catwalks, and a scenery fly loft and offstage areas will make provision of a properly designed concert shell mandatory. The stage is one area where meeting the needs of both music and drama requires foresight and care in the planning. Figure 3 shows the rigging needed for a music/drama auditorium.

Orchestra/Band Shell

If the auditorium has a traditional proscenium stage, it must have an adequate shell to be used for music. Room for shell storage also must be provided. The purpose of the shell is to project the sound into the audience for lectures, recitals, and music concerts. It conserves acoustic energy and directs it out to the listeners. It also has many benefits to those on stage whose intercommunication is enhanced, whose dynamic range is in-creased, and whose tone quality and blend are improved. Shells are discussed in greater detail in Chapter 5, page 49.

Budgeting for Equipment

Nowhere in a music facility is there likely to be so much latitude in the type and cost of equipment as there is on the stage. Unfortunately, there have been many projects where an auditorium and stage have been planned without adequate budgeting for the stage systems that are essential to their proper function.

COURTESY WENGER CORPORATION

Atlanta (Georgia) Symphony and Chorus
An acoustical shell is essential for music performed on a proscenium stage.

Figure 3. Stage Rigging System for a Music/Drama Auditorium

Rigging Required for	Remarks
Safety Curtains	Required only in proscenium spaces; may be omitted in certain instances, such as when a flood system is included (check fire code)
Light Battens	Required only in proscenium spaces (catwalks take the place of battens in open stage spaces)
Concert Shell	Required only in proscenium spaces; motorized battens desirable; often only shell ceiling is flown
Lightbridges and Heavy Weights	Motorized battens are best
Cyclorama and Stage Pieces	Required only in proscenium spaces; counterweight line sets and other rope sets are essential (rope sets not required in open stage performance spaces, but they do add flexibility)

These are major expense items that should be accepted from the beginning. Stage systems requiring special design and budgetary consideration are theatre lighting, control, and instruments; stage rigging; stage curtains and sound reflecting panels; band/orchestra/choir acoustical shell; orchestra pit (stage lift); sound system and recording; and projection equipment. An experienced theatre consultant can provide budget figures for these systems. Overlooking any of them in the planning, and adding them on later, always costs more and penalizes most of the activities carried on in the auditorium because of the unresolvable compromises that add-on systems always bring about.

Offstage Areas

Connected ancillary spaces to the stage must provide adequate storage for stage sets, sound panels, stage risers, music racks, and other paraphernalia connected with concert and drama presentations. The special backstage facilities needed for drama—scene shop, costume shop, properties room, rehearsal rooms, green rooms, special dressing rooms, and other areas—are outside the scope of this book. In a multipurpose auditorium, however, careful planning of proper storage facilities is especially important so that changeovers from music groups to play production is as easy as possible. Music ensembles preparing concerts, and drama groups readying plays, may need access to the stage during the same time periods a week to a month before performance. Orderly and sufficient storage space close to the stage will help ease scheduling conflicts and promote efficient use of the auditorium.

The Orchestra Pit

Musical theatre and opera represent an acoustically difficult marriage of instruments and voices. Particularly in educational and semiprofessional performances, instrumental sound tends to overwhelm voices. The orchestra pit is a necessary acoustical design element to help overcome the balance problems inherent in these situations. Closed-circuit television and creative scenery design can open other performing locations for the orchestra. However, the pit remains the most suitable overall location, and every auditorium that hopes to accommodate music theatre, ballet, or opera should include one. The critical parameters in pit design are area, configuration, and treatment.

Fifteen square feet per musician is a reasonable planning guide that assumes a performing group of greater than twenty-five musicians, including piano and percussion. For any facility that is to accommodate opera or ballet, a pit area of no less than 1,000 square feet should be provided. This will accommodate 60 to 75 musicians, depending on instrumentation.

In order for the conductor to see and be seen by both pit musicians and on-stage performers, the depth of the pit must be no greater than 7½ to 8 feet below stage level. To achieve adequate area for musicians while not cutting too deeply into the audience area, the space under the stage apron frequently is used. This space should not exceed 6 feet in depth and should have a height of 6½ feet clear. This implies that the thickness of the stage floor overhanging the pit should not exceed 12 inches. A length-to-width ratio of 2:1 or less is desirable to maintain reasonable balance and ensemble. In no case, however, should the width of the opening be less than 9 to 10 feet, nor the length

An orchestra pit should be provided for music theatre and opera.

greater than 55 to 60 feet. If at all possible, the orchestra pit platform should be mechanized.

Controlling loudness of the pit orchestra while maintaining a well-balanced sound projection presents a sensitive design problem. Since the upstage wall of the pit acts as an acoustic mirror reflecting sound energy to the audience, covering it with adjustable or permanent sound-absorbing treatment has considerable effect on the loudness perceived by an audience on the main floor. To the extent that the performers themselves are more visible, listeners in the balcony experience less change with this treatment than those on the main floor.

A railing with solid infill, all or part of which can be removed, is required on the audience side of the pit to shield the first few rows of listeners from being overwhelmed by pit sound. The railing further serves to aid communication by reflecting pit sound to onstage performers. Absorptive treatment of this wall should be avoided. Additional loudness control frequently can be achieved, and some blending and fullness developed, by coupling the pit volume with the volume of the seating wagon storage area located under the first few rows of audience seating. Coupling with the trap room under the stage also may serve this function. In addition to these acoustical needs, there are many other factors that must be considered, including access from the pit to warm-up rooms, dressing rooms, and so forth; storage of seating wagons if the pit doubles as an audience seating area; storage of pianos and percussion instruments; pit cover design if mechanization is not feasible; and use of the pit lift as a large freight elevator to connect lower level areas with the stage.

The orchestra pit should be tied into the house intercommunication system, with stations backstage and to the front of the house. Orchestra music racks are available that are designed for theatrical purposes, are large enough to hold unusual sizes of manuscript paper, and have built-in lights that strike the paper at an angle that permits little light to spill over. The pit should have enough outlets installed in the floor and along the walls to accommodate the maximum size orchestra, with the circuits controlled from the stage lighting control board.

Stage Manager's Desk

Every well-equipped auditorium should include provisions for a stage manager. While some of the stage manager's functions can be performed from control areas in the rear of an auditorium, the job can be performed best from a castered reading desk located on the side of the stage from which conductor and soloist enter, which is usually stage right. The stage manager sits on a comfortable stool and reads a script or cue sheet. He can communicate with performers and other technicians using a wall-mounted panel containing the desk cable outlet, a telephone handset, an electrical outlet, and a large clock synchronized with the clocks in the hall. The completely equipped stage manager's desk includes the following features:

1. Reading surface with retaining lip
2. Dimmer controlled reading light
3. House telephone or intercom master station
4. Paging master system
5. Cueing master station (N.B. Items 3, 4, and 5 can be combined into one system in less sophisticated installations)
6. Pit lift controls
7. Remote controls for concert, lecture, and house lights
8. Panic lighting control to throw house lights on in an emergency
9. Backstage worklight and rehearsal light control
10. Electrical outlet
11. Adjustable height stool with foot rail
12. Pencil sharpener
13. Coffee cup retaining ring
14. Locked drawer
15. 30-foot interconnect cable to wall panel (with means of coiling unused cable).

LOADING DOCK/ RECEIVING ROOM

Each performance hall must have an accessible loading dock for receiving equipment, with some space for temporary holding. Desirable features of the receiving area are:

1. Steps or a ramp for personnel access
2. Roof overhang for bad weather loading
3. Dock bumper for trucks
4. Loading door, a minimum of 8 feet wide and 8 feet high
5. At least 300 square feet of receiving space
6. Ramped or level access to backstage of the performance room, and to rehearsal, dressing, and stage storage rooms.

PUBLIC FACILITIES

Public Rooms

A common fault of school performing areas is that the lavatories and public rooms often are quite distant from the auditorium. In some instances, they are in parts of the building that are locked, so that there is no access to them during evening performances. The lounge facilities to accommodate the public between acts or during intermission should be large enough for comfort. The lounges and lobbies may be as luxurious as finances permit. The ventilating system should be separated from that of the theatre proper. An ideal and economical arrangement that can work well is one in which corridors, drinking fountains, and other facilities serve the student body during the

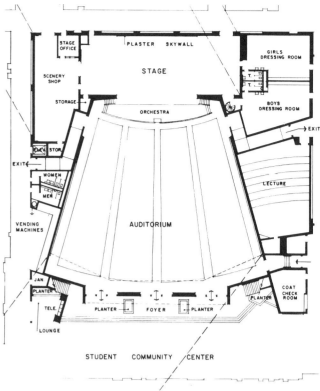

North Central High School, Indianapolis, Indiana
Architects: Everett I. Brown Company
Corridors, drinking fountains, and other facilities can be located to serve the students during the day and the audience in the evening.

day and the audience at evening functions, thus eliminating the need for double facilities. Such multiple use should be kept in mind in locating areas that will serve the public, but it never should be the prime factor achieved at the expense of other important considerations in a good layout. Signs should indicate clearly where ticket office, public telephone, and other public facilities are located. Audiences at evening events are infrequent visitors compared to the regular school students. Indicating clearly to them the location of conveniences they may wish to use is a matter of common courtesy that easily is overlooked. For audience recall after intermission, bells, chimes, a sound system to carry voice announcements, or a system for flashing lights in lobby areas should be provided.

Entrances and Exits

Auditoriums must be planned with adequate exits. The flow of pedestrian traffic to the ticket office, into the auditorium, and to or from parking facilities also must be considered. Cloakrooms should be convenient to building entrances, yet located where a line-up for wraps will not block exits or interfere with the orderly emptying of the auditorium.

Provision for Handicapped Persons

Those persons who must attend public events in a wheelchair now are being given more consideration, and recent building codes establish guidelines that must be followed. Ramps should be used instead of steps in at least one direct route to spaces where wheelchairs can be parked conveniently. The best location for wheelchairs is at the rear of the main floor out of the flow of audience traffic, perhaps separated from it with low temporary or permanent railings, and with direct access to the lobby or hallway for emergency exit. The path from the street to these wheelchair positions must be checked from time to time in the planning process to ensure that no obstacles have developed. It is important that wheelchair positions be determined at the time seating and sightlines are developed for the entire audience area. People with hearing handicaps will appreciate receptacles with individual volume controls into which they can plug special earphones for lectures, films, and other amplified speech activities.

AUDITORIUM SAFETY

Recommended practice includes use of aisle and step lights whenever the hall is darkened for plays or movies. Exit lights are standard. Some provision for emergency lighting in case of power failure also must be included. A standby battery system is probably the least expensive system that offers enough light for safety. Stage areas will have to be provided with automatic sprinklers in case of fire. The width of the aisles and the dimensions of the steps and risers are also safety considerations that come under the fire and building codes of each state or municipality. Onstage safety precautions, such as using steel (not rope)

cables on all stage rigging, supplying safety lines, and installing rails on risers all are sensible. Public liability is a matter of concern to every school board or board of trustees operating a public auditorium. Contracts for nonschool use of the facilities must be drawn carefully to require insurance by the user and absolve the school of any public liability. Such contracts should be drawn by the school attorney. The auditorium staff is expected to follow common sense in maintaining uncluttered catwalks, securing suspended panels and lights, and making sure emergency systems are kept in operating order.

MANAGING THE AUDITORIUM

Teams planning an auditorium often fail to look ahead to its scheduling and actual operation. The auditorium is likely to be a busy place, and one individual must have responsibility for maintaining a schedule book; contracting with nonschool users; invoicing and collecting for such uses; providing needed equipment and technical staff; overseeing adjustable features in a multipurpose auditorium; supervising maintenance; arranging for ushers, ticket takers, and parking supervisors for public events; and managing all the other details that need to be handled properly for the hall to realize its full service potential. This is done best by having a building manager with an office convenient to both the public and the school, or by assigning these responsibilities to someone on the office staff.

Chapter 5: Technical Considerations

Designing a music facility is a specialized task that taxes the capabilities of the school staff as well as those of many architectural offices. This is especially true in the area of technical considerations. Careful planning in this regard may yield larger dividends than in any other aspect of the building, and it is here that the specialized services of trained and experienced consultants can be used to best advantage. This is true even if the facility is to be a modest one. There are many pitfalls that an experienced adviser can avoid. It is quite common for such consultants to save more than enough money on a project to pay their fees. Most architects realize this and will advise that the consultants be hired.

In approaching the design of a music building, two basic technical problems must be faced. First, adequate isolation must be provided between various spaces for satisfactory simultaneous use. Second, satisfactory room acoustics must be provided for performers and listeners. These two objectives are achieved by *completely* different mechanisms. Isolation is achieved by the construction that separates two spaces, while room acoustics are determined by the shape and surface of the finishing materials used in the interior. There is often a misconception, for example, that the addition of sound-absorbing curtains on a wall will improve the isolation of sound from an adjoining space. It will do nothing but deaden the room itself, and will have very little effect on the amount of sound coming through from the next room.

SOUND ISOLATION

Sound isolation is concerned with the containment of sounds within the space where they are generated or in keeping unwanted sounds out. The intrusion of external sounds or the noise of a ventilating system can be destructive to activities carried on in a music room or auditorium. Consequently, the requirements for effective sound isolation should be given primary consideration. The areas of sound isolation and acoustics both are the responsibility of the acoustical consultant. The effect of different types of wall construction on the isolation of adjoining music rooms can be heard clearly on the soundsheet "Acoustics for the Music Educator" that accompanies this book (see inside back cover), and the reader may wish to listen to these examples in the context of the discussion that follows.

The degree of sound isolation required for various spaces in a music building will vary with the type of use. The most critical isolation problem probably is that for teaching studios and classrooms. Any audible musical sound has musical intelligibility, as contrasted with speech, which transmits as a vague mumble. This is especially important in classrooms used for music theory, where any audibility of musical sound from an adjoining room during music dictation is most disconcerting. Score reading and composition also require inaudibility of sounds from adjoining spaces. Practice rooms have less critical sound-isolation requirements, although even these will not be really satisfactory unless more than the usual classroom separation is provided. Large rehearsal rooms and recital halls often can be placed in separate units and achieve the isolation they require almost automatically. While one could conceive of a music building in which the isolation for all spaces could be achieved by widely separating all the rooms on a single level, this is hardly practical. Spaces should be conveniently related to each other, and this means that ways must be found for providing the required isolation between closely adjoining rooms.

Effective sound isolation between rooms is given by heavy, airtight walls, floors, and ceiling construction systems—the heavier the better. There is a limit, however, to how much isolation can be achieved in a typical building. No matter how heavy a wall is made, some sound will travel through the floor and ceiling slabs to adjoining spaces on the same level. The isolation limit set by these flanking paths is too low for the critical spaces in a music building. More complex constructions than those usually satisfactory in classroom buildings are therefore mandatory. One can achieve very high values of sound isolation in a concrete building only by floating an inner skin (walls, floors, and ceilings) for each of the spaces within the basic structure. The structure of the building must be protected from airborne and structure-borne sound waves by the addition of a resiliently separated layer of plaster or concrete. A discussion of this complex type of structure with an architect almost always elicits the question, "Isn't there some simpler way of doing it?" The answer is, "Unfortunately, no." This type of floated interior construction also gives isolation from the structure-borne sound of pianos, cellos, and other instruments that drive the floor directly.

The needs for such high sound isolation preclude the possibility of using natural ventilation. *A music building must be air-conditioned throughout, and air must be supplied through sound-absorbent, lined ductwork and returned through lined ductwork*, possibly incorporating silencers if lengths of ductwork

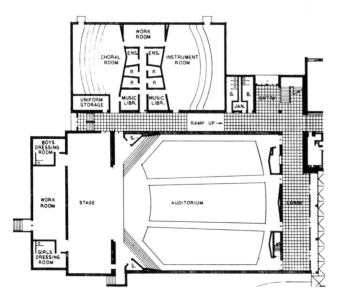

Solon (Ohio) High School
Architects: Dela Motte, Larson, Nassau & Associates
Large rehearsal rooms and recital halls can be placed in separate units to achieve sound isolation.

between spaces are inadequate. Door louvers and other usual ventilating practices cannot be used here. While the isolated interior skin of the room may be shaped to serve the purposes of good room acoustics, it must be heavy, continuous, and not shortcircuited to the basic structure of the building by electrical conduit, ventilating ducts, or any other rigid path. The details of windows and doors are not easy, but they must be worked out in each case. These problems can be solved if the designer is willing to take the trouble. The investment in added cost of construction will not be realized in adequate sound isolation, however, unless every single detail is solved in the design and is seen through carefully to completion. It is helpful to instruct workmen in the reasoning behind the fussy construction system and the necessity of avoiding any accidental bridges between the floated interior and the basic structure of the building. Even so, supervision by a knowledgeable person during the actual construction of these critical areas is imperative. A music building incorporating this specialized kind of construction will be much more expensive than a normal classroom building—as much as twice as expensive.

Practice rooms often can be handled more simply in terms of isolation, but they, too, require supply and return of air through lined ductwork and the use of weatherstripped doors—perhaps less expensive ones than those used in teaching studios and classrooms. This assumes that there will be some audibility of sound from an adjoining room when no sound is being made in a given room, but that it won't be enough to disturb a person who is practicing an instrument.

Even when the complex type of construction just described is used, there still may be some audible musical sound from the next space if the background sound level is very low. In addition to the sound-isolating construction, there also must be a moderate background noise level in teaching and practice spaces. This usually means counting on the air conditioning system for slightly audible amounts of air noise. In air-conditioning terms, this is a background noise spectrum of NC 30-35. Such a background noise will in no way interfere with normal activities in teaching spaces and will very effectively mask or conceal the tiny amounts of sound energy that inevitably intrude with even the best construction. Such a masking background also can be useful in the music library to hide both speech and musical intrusions from other activities there. Music listening rooms associated with the library need the same sort of construction as teaching studios, including the moderate continuous background noise. Because mechanical systems are at times unpredictable or erratic, it may be helpful to generate the masking sound electronically. Recital halls, auditoriums, and any space to be used for recording or music performance must be completely free of noise; absolutely no masking noise can be tolerated there.

No matter how effective the sound-isolating construction between spaces may be, the overall isolation achieved always will be better if there is no insistence on such difficult relationships as rehearsal rooms over recital halls or heavy mechanical equipment under the stage of the auditorium. Isolation can be achieved in such situations, but it always costs more than when it is possible to separate these elements more widely in the building. Single story, on-grade construction actually provides the most practical and least expensive isolation for music wings under many conditions and always should be considered first.

Sound-absorbing treatments should be used in all corridors and lobbies to minimize the transmission of sound, and as many doors as possible should be closed between rooms to be isolated from each other. No amount of corridor treatment is as effective as a closed door. Doors to all isolated rooms must be of special sound-isolating construction, and they must be fully weatherstripped on all four edges. Any leaks or cracks, no matter how small, will nullify the effectiveness of these doors. The weatherstrips must be maintained and adjusted from time to time to keep them airtight. Even the best acoustical doors available today are not as effective in containing sound within a room as are well-designed and carefully constructed walls, and it is a mistake to expect them to be so. Glass vision panels in a door or glass wall panels can weaken the sound-isolating capabilities, too, unless they are double-glazed with a deep airspace between, properly installed, and carefully sealed. In critical areas, they should be avoided if at all possible.

Use of a sound lock at entrances to practice areas, rehearsal rooms, or auditoriums often is advisable. A sound lock consists of two separate doors with a vestibule between them. In an area devoted to practice rooms or teaching studios, it seldom is considered worthwhile to install two doors, even though single well-sealed doors still will permit appreciable sound transmission to the corridors. From one practice room to another, there always will be two doors in the path, and room-to-corridor isolation is not critical. A word of caution is in order here about the so-called soundproof or acoustical doors on the market. Test results always are based on ideal installations under laboratory conditions, and should not be taken too literally. Obviously, wood doors must be solid rather than hollow core. If compression-type gasketing systems are used, they must be very soft and easily compressed. Packages are available that include the doors and the gasketing system, and these tend to be more acceptable than separate ones. The desired performance must be specified carefully by the design team and not just designated as soundproof or weatherstripped. Drop seals tend to click and should be avoided in quiet performance spaces. Requiring performance specifications in which tests of the complete installation are made by the acoustics consultant before the installation is accepted by the owner will assure satisfactory performance. Quality of installation is so important that such performance specifications may be the only way of assuring adequate performance. Unless this is done, money for special doors may have been wasted.

ACOUSTICS

Attention to the acoustics environment is important in every building, but this aspect must be particularly well handled in a music building. Without good conditions for performance, rehearsal, teaching, composing, or reading, a music building simply cannot provide the environment for good teaching. The soundsheet "Acoustics for the Music Educator" in back of this book demonstrates these points aurally and should be referred to here. Acoustics, like structure, air conditioning, and lighting, must be considered from the very beginning of building planning. Although sensible planning and arrangement of spaces sometimes can obviate the need for expensive sound-isolating construction, a music building always will cost more than an ordinary classroom building. Unfortunately, there are no shortcuts to the achievement of satisfactory conditions. It either *is* or *is not* a good music facility. Satisfactory acoustics is more than providing a space free from obvious acoustic faults, and it is more than isolating sound from surrounding areas when sound is not wanted. The acoustic properties of a room can enhance the quality of music for the listener and can give the performer a sense of support that adds to the pleasure and quality of his performance.

Room Acoustics

After the required isolation has been provided, it must be determined how these isolated spaces sound to their occupants.

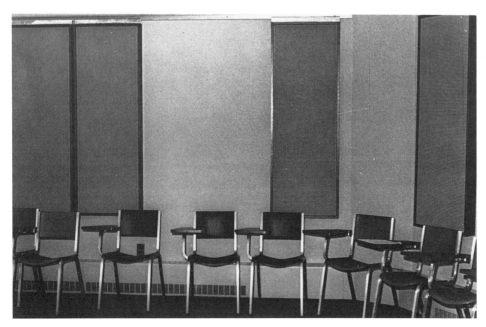

Left: Individual panels of absorptive material can be hung from picture moldings to provide adjustable room acoustics.

Right: Bridgman (Michigan) High School
Architects: Daverman Associates
Acoustics: Harold Geerdes
Flutter echo problems can be controlled by angling the walls and using irregular surfaces.

The acoustics problems in small practice rooms, and even in medium or large rehearsal rooms, are quite different from those in large recital halls and auditoriums: it is impossible to make them sound alike, as architects often are asked to do. The acoustics of a good auditorium enhance the beauty and balance of the sound. A good rehearsal room in an educational facility, on the other hand, is designed to fulfill its function best as a teaching station; clarity and focus on individuals are important if precision, intonation, and other fundamentals of musicianship are to be analyzed and improved. This work is carried on less effectively in a reverberant auditorium than in a well-designed rehearsal room. For musicians with a high degree of proficiency, this factor is less important, but it is nevertheless a relevant consideration at the school and college level.

Spaces that vary in size will vary in sound, and their treatments must differ accordingly. An undertreated small room can be loud, harsh, muddy, and quite unacceptable for any music uses. The reverberation time in a small studio must be considerably lower than that considered ideal for a large rehearsal room. Because sound travels at the same speed in all spaces, the separation between successive reflections of sound becomes greater in larger rooms.

In the small practice room or teaching studio, there are stronger resonant frequencies in the audible range that must be suppressed. In some cases, the control of these resonances may require that the room have certain proportions of dimension. In larger rooms, where the predominant resonances are at sub-audible frequencies, proportions become less important than basic requirements for height and width. Sound-absorbing materials in a small music room generally are required on at least two adjacent walls and the ceiling. These materials should be effective throughout the full frequency range. Acoustic tile glued to a ceiling is not as effective in the low and middle frequency ranges as is a suspended lay-in system. For reverberation control, either a sound-absorbing ceiling or fully-carpeted floor can be incorporated. A curtain track along one wall allows a heavy drapery to be either extended across one wall or pushed back into the corner to vary the reverberant characteristics of the space. These are matters of individual taste and preference, and one cannot predict in advance what an individual is likely to prefer. Because of this, facilities may incorporate a flexible acoustical system into practice rooms and teaching studios. This involves the installation of special one-inch picture moldings on all the walls, from which individual panels of absorptive mate-

rial can be hung. These panels can be made inexpensively in a school shop out of 1 x 4-inch lumber, filled with fiberglass sheets, and covered with fabric. Each studio thus can be somewhat custom-treated to suit the requirements of each teacher and each space. Some on-the-spot experimenting over a period of time is then possible. A hard-finished small room will be liked by no one, and a room completely padded with sound-absorbing material also is unlikely to be appreciated.

Flutter echo or ring, caused by the reflection of sound back and forth between parallel surfaces, can be avoided by installing absorptive treatments to eliminate hard opposing parallel surfaces or by avoiding the parallelism itself. It can be avoided either by skew or tilt of the walls, or by such added devices as tilted blackboards, bookcases filled with many objects, or modulation of the wall surfaces with large irregularities. Almost any architectural device that destorys the smooth parallelism of two wall surfaces will eliminate flutter echo.

Whether the room is finished in plaster or wood is a matter of individual preference, and a wide variation of treatments can produce acceptable results. Small practice rooms and studios can be made comfortable to the occupant, and exterior windows here are acceptable. The prefabricated practice rooms mentioned in Chapter 4 already have incorporated all required acoustic treatment.

Left: The Juilliard School, New York City
Architect: Pietro Belluschi
Associated Architects: Eduardo Catalano and Helge Westerman
Organ studios require special acoustical consideration.

Below: The Juilliard School, New York City
Architect: Pietro Belluschi
Associated Architects: Eduardo Catalano and Helge Westermann
Large areas of heavy drapes on two adjacent walls provide acoustic flexibility in instrumental rehearsal rooms

EZRA STOLLER

Organ Studios

Rooms for teaching or practicing the organ call for special consideration unless they are for the small electronic instruments that can be accommodated satisfactorily in a regular practice room. Pipe organs are found in increasing numbers in college studios. Unless they are planned with care, however, studios for organ can be inadequate. The first consideration must be the physical size of the instrument. Organ consoles, pipework, chests, and action vary considerably, and many of them require more space than is found in a piano practice room. For accoustical reasons, the organ studio should be large enough in volume to provide the instrument with space to speak out properly. It should be hard-surfaced but with some acoustical flexibility so the organist can adjust the dryness or reverberance of the room to suit his preferences. The larger the volume given to the instrument, the better. If scheduling permits, the planner even may consider placing the practice instruments in music classrooms to take advantage of the volume available.

Classrooms

Large classrooms do not have the problem of low-frequency resonance because the principal resonances will be below the audible range. It still is important, however, to avoid flutter echoes between parallel wall surfaces and to control the reverberation time with adequate treatment on wall and ceiling surfaces. Fairly extensive treatments are needed to ensure that the low-frequency reverberation is not too long, but that there is still some life in the room to enhance the quality of musical sound. Placing acoustical tile on the entire ceiling, as is done in other classrooms, is not conducive to the best sound for music teaching. The ratio of reflective to absorptive material depends on the size and shape of the room, among other factors, and is best left to the judgment of the acoustical consultant.

Rehearsal Areas

Large rehearsal rooms for instrumental groups and for choruses often suffer from inadequate volume. A large instrumental rehearsal room should have at least a two-story ceiling for satisfactory conditions. Here, as in the teaching studios and classrooms, parallel hard wall surfaces should be avoided. The sound-absorbing treatment needed to control reverberation can be incorporated in the wall areas to help achieve this dispersion. The ceiling should have a mixture of sound-absorbing and sound-reflecting surfaces to enable the musicians to hear each other. Rehearsal rooms should not be too reverberant in order that the faulty performers can be identified and corrected readily. As in teaching studios, large areas of heavy drapery sometimes are provided for extension across one or two walls to vary the characteristics of the room. It also will make the room serve better the needs of both band and orchestra, since a more reverberant room is needed for orchestra rehearsal than for band. The installation of the curtain, which is most effective if made of heavy velour with special liner, should be included in the original building budget.

The use of carpeting in rehearsal rooms (see Chapter 3, page 12) does little if anything to counter the loudness and boominess that are the greatest threats to good rehearsal room sound. These factors are better controlled by fixed sound-absorbing treatment of much greater depth than carpeting provides. Placing absorption so close to the performer is unnatural and encourages forcing in tone production. Placing carpet under the percussion section to reduce its sound level makes some sense, as does sound-absorbing treatment close to them on the walls. But most players will hear themselves and the other performers better on a hard, reflective floor surface.

Good sound distribution is as important as reverberation time in a rehearsal room, and it is a factor that often is minimized in the design. So is the need for broad-band sound absorption—not just that provided by carpeting or glued-on ceiling tile, both of which have little value in giving the room a flat response that is free of boominess. A wide variety of solutions is available to the architect, and the exact treatment selected will depend on budget, the needs of the individual situation, and the expertise of the acoustical adviser. If the rehearsal room is to be used for some recording purposes, good acoustics, quiet lighting and ventilating systems, and enough volume for good musical sound become critical design considerations, although rehearsal rooms generally are too dead for serious recording.

Recital Halls

The recital hall generally seats from 200 to 300 people and is used not only for performances but also for rehearsal. The recital hall should have an adequate ceiling height to provide the volume required for proper reverberation time. If an organ is incorporated, it may be desirable to provide heavy draperies to lower the reverberation time for piano and other instruments requiring a less live space. The chairs in the recital hall always should be fabric upholstered (never vinyl) to give a reasonably constant reverberation time regardless of occupancy. The hall should be more or less rectangular; circular forms should be avoided. The walls and ceiling surfaces should provide a high degree of sound diffusion through irregularities. The stage area, in particular, should be designed for good reflection of sound to the audience as well as to other performers on stage. The ceiling height above the performing platform should not exceed 20 feet—it can be a little less than this—and the walls surrounding the platform should be skewed to avoid parallelism. Some people express a prejudice for using wood as the finish treatment in such a hall, but equally satisfactory results can be had with plaster. The old-fashioned rococo rooms with heavily coffered ceilings, walls treated with niches and statuary, and irregularities of all sorts almost inevitably resulted in good sound. Now ways must be found in a contemporary idiom to achieve these results. The background noise from the air conditioning system and from other spaces should be inaudible in the recital hall. Here, a masking noise would reduce audibility of sound. Making the air conditioning system quiet is not easy, but it can be done.

Auditoriums

The large auditorium, whether it is designed purely as a concert hall or as a multipurpose auditorium, poses problems considerably more difficult than those of the small rehearsal rooms or recital halls. If its proposed uses indicate that fairly long reverberation times (two seconds) are desirable, as for organ and choral music, this immediately will demand a rather large vol-

ume for the space. Such an auditorium should not be much larger than 2000 or 2500 seats. Although larger successful auditoriums have been built, the problems of achieving satisfactory acoustics become much greater, and their solutions require costly treatment that usually is not justified in educational situations.

Various seating arrangements for the audience have been discussed in Chapter 4. Fortunately, good sightlines also mean good hearing-lines, and a steeply raked floor is helpful to good sound as well as sight. Deep underbalcony spaces must be avoided, and every listener must be able not only to see the performers, but also to receive reflected sound from a good part of the upper wall and ceiling area. Careful balancing of sightline and acoustic requirements determines the seating geometry, which in turn determines the gross volume of the space for the achievement of the desired reverberation time. It also will determine the reflections needed from various surfaces in the hall to achieve intimacy and clarity as well as overall fullness and warmth.

Almost inevitably, the main ceiling of the auditorium is quite high over the forward section of seating. This makes it necessary to add other reflecting surfaces at a lower height to give the required intimacy and clarity that come from early reflection of sound to the listener. The balance between the amount of early sound (that received directly from the source and that from reflections within the first 30 to 40 milliseconds after the original sound arrives at the ear) and the reverberant field that gives a sense of fullness and warmth must be worked out carefully. If there is too much early sound, there may not be enough body. Conversely, if there is not enough early sound, lack of definition and clarity will result. A good balance can be achieved, but its attainment will dictate certain architectural details in the design of the auditorium.

Gymnasiums

A discussion of music performance areas should not have to include any rooms that compromise performance. However, many educational institutions, especially elementary schools, have no auditorium. In these schools, music departments must make all of their public presentations in the school athletic facility. Most gymnasiums, because of their large volume and hard, reflective surfaces, are excessively muddy and boomy, and their stages invariably are inadequate. Lighting designed for catching basketballs seldom is fit for reading sixteenth notes, and provision for special stage lighting or for dimming audience circuits usually is not made. The audience does not have customary amenities, such as comfortable seating. Noisy ventilating systems usually must be turned off during concerts, to the discomfort of both performers and listeners.

In spite of this, many music festivals and concert performances are conducted each year in such inadequate spaces. The director faced with this unpleasant reality should make the best of it and not just accept the status quo. Even with considerable attention to acoustics, lighting, and so forth, playing or singing in a gymnasium never will equal performance in a good auditorium. However, it often can be made less intolerable if the problems encountered are analyzed and an attempt is made to minimize them. If an inadequate stage makes performance on the gymnasium floor necessary, a portable acoustic shell and portable staging (which is helpful for acoustical as well as visual reasons) will enhance the performance considerably, particularly if foresight was shown in the original planning and the ceiling and some side walls have tectum or other sound-absorbing materials on them. A cantilevered shell with built-in downlights provides lighting similar to that of an auditorium stage and also offers better sound reflection than the smaller, portable music shell. Acoustic consultants can help plan not only the new gymnasium, but also can help make an existing one less hostile for music.

SHELLS

Unless it has an open stage, a multipurpose hall rarely can serve music well without an acoustical enclosure for band, orchestra, choir, and other music performances. This is a fundamental requirement that must receive careful attention in the early planning and budgeting. Finding the expertise and the money to provide a proper shell later usually is nearly impossible. Thousands of performances each year are given in auditoriums built without this basic provision for staging concerts. They never can realize their full potential for either performers or listeners.

A stage enclosure is an *essential* part of a multipurpose auditorium that has any kind of stage house. It cannot be considered a piece of optional stage equipment without disastrous results to any kind of music performance. No music organization can per-

Above: Bellevue (Washington
    Community College
Architects: Naramore, Bain,
    Brady & Johnson
Acoustics: Robin M. Towne
    Associates, Inc.
This gymnasium was designed for athletic functions, student assemblies, and musical programs. It incorporates a high degree of acoustical correction to make it an acceptable space for music.

Left: University of North
    Dakota, Grand Forks
Music performances in gymnasiums can be enhanced by the use of portable staging, risers, and acoustic shells.

form effectively on a stage draped with velour. The musicians simply will not be able to hear themselves or each other, the projection of the sound to the audience will be inadequate, and if the hall is a live one acoustically, the onstage and offstage sounds will be completely unlike. A first requirement for good auditorium acoustics is appropriate coupling of sound qualities on the sending end and the receiving end (see Figure 4).

Design criteria for the shell must grow out of the musical requirements of the performers who will use the facility and the characteristics of the facility itself. If it is to serve the community symphony orchestra, as many school auditoriums do, the shell should be as sophisticated as the community can afford. For school use, the design should not be compromised severely if the best musical results are desired, but there are cost-cutting approaches that still will produce satisfactory results. Acoustical design considerations include energy conservation (to overcome losses due to sound absorption and sound transmission), on-stage balance (to equalize upstage-downstage levels and improve intercommunication between players), general size, and configuration. In addition, there are theatrical factors that influence the design of an enclosure, including construction methods and materials, operation and mobility, storage and maintenance, lighting, and safety.

If a shell is added to an existing auditorium, light battens may fall between ceiling panels. In some cases, this even may be desirable in a new auditorium. Generally, however, the shell should not attempt to use border lights but should have lights installed in each section of the ceiling so that the stage will be flooded with a minimum of 70 footcandles of lighting. The lights should be arranged so that the back row will have sufficient light and should be angled 15 to 18 degrees so the lights will not throw a glare back into the audience. Front

lighting may be used for fill only. The shell should be the full width of the proscenium. The ceiling can hang from the battens. The size of the shell can be varied by adding or subtracting flats and adding or subtracting ceiling sections. Its design should be entrusted to the acoustical consultant.

When an enclosure is provided, it should be designed so that its erection or removal is simple and quick. This almost always means mechanization of the handling system, although some manually operated enclosures have given good results. The enclosure in a stagehouse usually should be fairly tight, with a minimum of openings to the backstage area. It should have sound diffusing surfaces and, if possible, some of these should be adjustable to permit various arrangements of performing groups and balance between sections. If the ceiling is more than 25 feet above the performers, there may be difficulty in onstage hearing. There are no miracle materials for enclosures. As in the case of sound isolation, the weight of the enclosure material will determine its reflectivity to the full sound spectrum.

A variation in auditorium design that permits music performances without having a stage enclosure is one in which the ensemble performs in the front part of the hall before a hard backdrop (usually an asbestos curtain or a special sound-reflecting screen) and uses the forward part of the auditorium walls and ceiling as its reflectors. This means that the capacity of the auditorium is reduced when used for orchestral performances, but it does minimize the amount of backstage setup work required to give the musicians a good performing environment.

An enclosure or shell also is required whenever music is performed outdoors. The same general principles govern the design of these outdoor enclosures. The once-popular semicircular or parabolic forms for these shells never should be used. Any form of concave geometry will focus certain parts of the performing

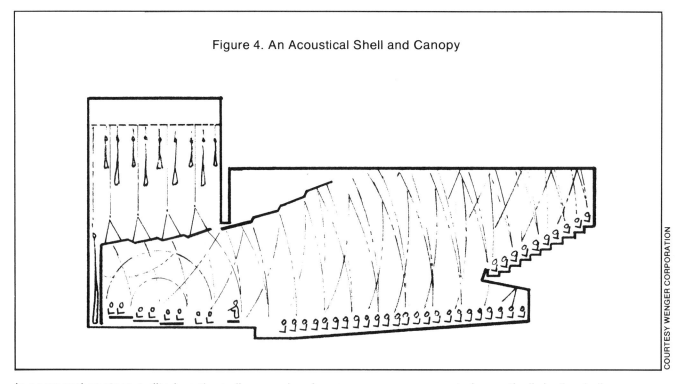

Figure 4. An Acoustical Shell and Canopy

COURTESY WENGER CORPORATION

In a proscenium stage auditorium, the audience and performance areas are connected acoustically by the shell or canapy.

Miller Outdoor Theatre, Houston, Texas
An enclosure is required whenever music is performed outdoors.

group toward certain parts of the audience in an undesirable way.

An orchestra enclosure always should be made of surfaces with modulations to encourage sound diffusion and more uniform distribution. The exact shape of such an enclosure is determined by the geometry of the seating area as well as the size and nature of the performing groups. The greater the extension of the enclosure's ceiling out over the audience, the better will be the result. Shells can be built of wood, concrete, steel, fiberglass-reinforced plastic, or any reasonably dense, well-damped sound-reflecting material. For any specific design, there are optimum materials and configurations based on the special requirements of that facility.

VARIABLE ACOUSTICS

One of the unexpected benefits for the school music director who performs in a multipurpose auditorium with adjustable acoustics is the capability it gives him to vary the acoustical environment to suit music of different periods or performance by different ensembles. The same movable panels and curtains that are placed in the hall to make it usable for both speech and music also serve him in an exciting musical way if he is alert to the creative possibilities. Composers such as Bach and Gabrieli, for example, were very much aware of the acoustical ambience in which their music was to be performed, and it is probable that they would have written differently if their halls were different. A number of these halls still are in use—enough to indicate what the acoustics were like for Mozart, Beethoven, and many others. The adjustability built into a school auditorium offers a unique chance, formerly found only in some major concert halls, to perform the composer's music in an acoustical environment similar to that for which it was composed.[8]

[8]See Harold Geerdes, "Adjustable Acoustics in Music Performance," *Music Educators Journal*, Vol. 61, No. 8 (April 1975).

The adjustable features designed into a versatile school or college auditorium include some or all of the following:

1. A full stage enclosure that may incorporate movable forestage side panels and a movable removable ceiling

2. A portable shell

3. Adjustable sound-absorbing treatment on the sides and the rear wall surfaces and sometimes in the ceiling zone of the audience seating area

4. Stage curtains of different acoustical qualities

5. Operable ceilings to close off part of the seating area or change the volume of the hall. This last feature was incorporated into the Auditorium Theatre in Chicago at the turn of the century to close off the top balcony, and it has been successfully used in some recent auditoriums as well.

How can these adjustable features be used for music performance? A listing of some of the optimum acoustical conditions for different types of performances on a scale of dry to reverberant conditions follows:

1. Drama, lecture, movies — Dry
2. Band concerts
3. Piano recitals
4. Chamber music
5. Musical theatre
6. Opera
7. Orchestra concerts
8. Choir with orchestra
9. Choir alone
10. Organ — Reverberant

A parallel listing can be prepared for the music of various composers, ranging from moderately reperberant for Bach and Stravinsky to highly reverberant for Gabrieli. One need not be highly refined in doing this. It is relatively simple in an adjustable hall to extend the acoustical control curtains or adjust stage panels to absorb sound and reduce the reverberation time until the desired condition exists.

HEATING AND VENTILATING

The major problem in ventilating an auditorium is to move sufficient air without creating drafts or disturbing noise. Since windows are not desirable in an auditorium, all ventilating has to be mechanical. Most ventilating and air conditioning equipment is noisy, and too many auditoriums suffer from a high ambient noise level. Special engineering and installation practices are required, and maximum acceptable levels should be specified for each area, using the numbers of applicable Noise Criterion Curves. An NC of 15 is needed in a 1,000 seat auditorium, an NC of 25 in a rehearsal room or music classroom, and an NC of 30 or slightly above in a practice room or teaching studio where some masking sound is considered desirable.

Air conditioning equipment, cooling machinery, and ventilating fans should not be in close proximity to the auditorium. Ducts should contain acoustical lining as well as baffles to prevent the transmission of these machinery noises. The amount of air supplied backstage should not cause the front curtain to billow. There must be a balance of air between the stage supply and the auditorium supply, and between the stage exhaust and the auditorium exhaust. Drafts in an auditorium, on a stage, or in an orchestra pit are serious. They can affect stage scenery, affect the pitch of instruments, and cause discomfort to the audience. Keeping the noise level low can be accomplished in part by moving a large volume of air at low velocity. If grills are used on the supply ducts, they must not add noise and produce turbulence in the air. In critical areas, such as practice room suites, the ducts must have reverse paths and angles introduced in the duct layout to secure effective sound isolation even when adjacent rooms share the same air handling unit. A trained heating and ventilating engineer with auditorium and music room experience, working closely with the acoustics consultant, can meet the requirements for quietness without compromising the comfort of either the performers or the audience. An example of the effect of mechanical system noise on music can be heard on the soundsheet "Acoustics for the Music Educator," which accompanies this book (see inside back cover).

A good air-conditioning system includes humidity control, which is very important where pianos and wooden or string instruments are stored. Changes in humidity also can affect some of the percussion instruments. Humidity has an effect on acoustics, but just how and to what degree still is being studied. There is no disagreement, however, as to the desirability of year-round constant humidity in music storage, rehearsal, and performance areas.

ILLUMINATION

A well-designed environment must have lighting as another of its initial considerations. Good space relationships and the use of good materials in the music suite and auditorium may be negated by the wrong choice of lighting systems. Planning the fixtures and systems that will give the required number of footcandles for various activities should be done by the architect with the aid of a competent illuminating engineer or lighting consultant. Power and light companies and equipment manu-

Madeira School, Greenway, Virginia, lower floor plan
Architects: David N. Yerkes & Associates
Air conditioning and other mechanical equipment should not be located close to performance areas.

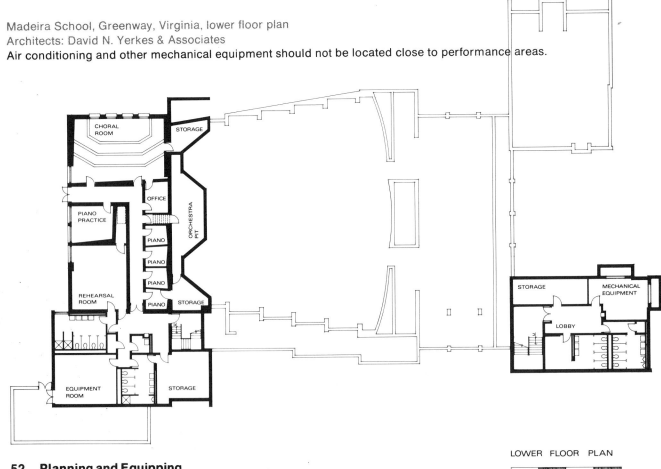

LOWER FLOOR PLAN

Figure 5. Recommended Reflectances

80-85%

WINDOW WALL
75-80%

30-40% TRIM

15-20% CHALKBOARD

50-60%
60-70% PERMISSIBLE WHEN
ENTIRE ROOM MEETS
RECOMMENDATION

35-50% DESK TOPS

30-40%

15-30% FLOOR

Recommended reflectances for finishes and furnishing in the classroom.

facturers are additional sources of information that can be valuable if used discretely. By coordinating the efforts of all of these sources, proper consideration can be given to visual needs, initial costs, energy costs, conservation, operation and maintenance costs, and architectural design. The result should help provide a satisfactory visual environment for all music teaching and performing areas, with adequate illumination in those specialized areas requiring it. This will not be achieved if the lighting is added after the entire architectural concept has been completed. It must be considered very carefully and planned as an integral, basic part of the design. Satisfactory lighting for the music department cannot be realized without an understanding of the visual problems encountered, and the architect should be made especially aware of them. Some of these considerations are:

1. In music rooms, small details are important. Lack of uniformity in manuscript, ink, and paper, as well as inconsistent size of music symbols and printing methods, adds to the difficulty.

2. The instrument played, and the necessity of sharing music, often result in awkward positioning of the music at an unusual distance from the eyes. Visual comfort and efficiency sometimes are sacrificed for appearance in adjusting music racks.

3. Musicians are expected to read rapidly and accurately while also following the conductor's motions.

4. Irregular seating arrangements force students to face the director from various angles and complicate the problems of glare and distracting objects entering the visual field.

5. Music rooms necessarily are equipped with furnishings that can create a condition of visual clutter.

6. Music, charts, or other materials to be viewed are displayed on a nearly vertical music rack where the light level is typically below that of the horizontal plane. Viewing often is from long range and at wide angles.

7. Musicians standing or sitting on the top platform have a different relationship with light sources located in the ceiling from those sitting at floor level or standing on a director's podium.

8. The angle of lighting is critical in performance situations where performers must look up at the conductor as well as view their music. This places certain strictures on the use of front lighting in an acoustical shell.

9. Music rooms are used day and night, summer and winter, for varied activities, some of which are nonmusical and have many different lighting requirements.

In addition to the above visual problems, the lighting system in any space devoted to the teaching, rehearsing, or performing of music must comply with rigid noise requirements.

Quality versus Quantity

Whether in a regular classroom or one used for music, comfortable, functional lighting depends more on the quality of an installation than the quantity of light in the space. The level of illumination must be sufficient in footcandles, but even more important is the elimination of direct and reflected glare, high contrast, and shadows. Attention should be paid to the following factors:

1. Controlling the illumination levels of visual tasks (footcandles).

2. Keeping brightness of light sources within acceptable levels (footlamberts).

3. Controlling contrast and brightness ratios (a) between light sources and ceiling, (b) between the printed page and the floor or walls, (c) between windows and walls, and (d) between music background and conductor background.

4. Providing proper diffusion through elimination of objectionable reflections, shadows, and bright spots.

Illumination levels for school tasks have been the subject of continuing research, as shown in publications such as *American Standard Practice for School Lighting* and Illuminating Engineering Society *Lighting Handbook*. A minimum of 30 footcandles for reading simple scores and 70 footcandles for complex scores is compatible with I.E.S. published standards. This would indicate that no less than 70 footcandles be provided by general illumination in the rehearsal room or on stage. If proper diffusion and good angles exist, this should be adequate for the performance. Some carefully-placed front lighting helps to soften shadows and improve the visual image for the audience. Flexibility in lighting levels and separate area controls enhance the enjoyment of audiences attending recitals and concerts, lectures, or film-showings, and is essential for drama, music theatre, and similar productions.

Brightness of the light source is determined by lighting fixture selection. Whatever the source, careful consideration should be given to the noise level and its dimming capability as well as to the proper selection of materials for diffusers, fixture housings, shielding louvres, and lenses. In every installation, the designer must take into account first costs, ease of maintenance, repair and replacement, size, appearance, color, and heating effect. Contrast and brightness ratios must be controlled to add visual comfort and efficiency. The brightness ratio between the music rack surfaces and the music should be limited to 3 to 1. This suggests lightly colored nonglaring finishes on the face of the rack. The music stand is usually in the field of vision of other players and should be finished to blend with the surroundings. The appearance of the stands and folios to the audience when the group appears in concert also is a factor to be considered. Woodwork and furnishings for music rooms should meet the recommended reflectance range. The floor should not be too dark. Green chalkboards easily are held in line with the recommended brightness ratio of the board to its wall background. Boards with higher than 20 percent reflectance reduce the contrast of chalk with board, and the visibility of chalk marks accordingly suffers. Steel chalkboards with fired abrasive enamel surfaces enable small magnets to be used to post bulletins or demonstrate marching band formations (see Figure 5).

Proper diffusion of light is a function of the type of shielding or materials used as diffusers on the fixtures themselves, the number and distribution of fixtures, and the selection of light-colored matte-finished materials for walls, furnishings, and

equipment that will reflect light without glare. This will help control reflected brightness, which is as much a problem as direct brightness.[9]

Natural versus Artificial

Unilateral daylighting from windows at one side of the room is included in many room plans. While popular and practical, it does involve a number of inherent problems:

1. Natural light is not dependable (cloudy days).

2. Sunlight is not available for evening and night rehearsals.

3. Students near the windows may have very high levels of light (100 footcandles or more), with levels falling off rapidly to the inside rows where there may be less than 5 footcandles on a bright day. Sky glare can be a problem.

4. Windows that serve some students well as a source of light are a source of glare and discomfort to the director or others in the room.

5. At night, windows usually become dark areas to those within the room. Proper shades are usually able to satisfy these last two considerations.

Multilateral (clerestory) daylighting can raise the ambient interior brightness to offset high indoor-outdoor contrast, especially if light-colored floors are used. With increased awareness of energy conservation, many architects are rediscovering daylight as a light source. However, without well-planned use of daylight, spaces may need more electric light during the day than at night, in order to overcome some of the problems mentioned above. Problems also can exist because of building orientation. Windows might be hit by direct sunlight instead of being protected by overhangs or sun control devices.

In many recent school designs, music rooms as well as lecture rooms and auditoriums have been built without windows. This can simplify the design of the lighting system. In addition to lighting considerations, there are other good arguments for the windowless room, such as easier control of the acoustical and thermal environment, easier adaptability for use of visual aids, and elimination of distractions. Proper uses of lighting, different building materials, and color can eliminate the claustrophobic atmosphere of such rooms.

Maintenance

Particular attention should be given to adequate maintenance of the lighting system. Without a planned program of periodic fixture cleaning and replacement of lamps, illumination levels can drop to half of the installed values. In auditoriums or other high-ceilinged rooms where scaffolding is required to replace lamps, it is more efficient to replace all lamps at one time. Lamp life can be predicted accurately and a relamping and cleaning program for the school planned for vacation periods at intervals that approach the useful life of the lamps. Maintenance crews must be instructed to replace lamps with ones of equivalent wattage and color or they will frustrate the carefully worked out levels of the lighting engineer.

Care always should be taken to relamp fluorescent fixtures with the proper color of lamps. Illumination levels as well as colors of walls are greatly affected by the choice of fluorescent

[9]Reflectance values of different color samples may be seen inside the back cover of the I.E.S. *Lighting Handbook* (5th Edition).

lamp color. The lumen output per watt of electricity (efficacy) is highest with cool white and warm white lamps. This is the primary reason most installations use these sources. However, recent developments in lamp design have produced lamps that have much better color rendition properties but lower efficiencies. The deluxe cool white lamp has the best color rendering (that is, nearest to natural daylight) and brings out colors of furnishings, clothing, and healthy-looking skin tones. Deluxe warm white lamps can be used where a much warmer atmosphere with good color rendering is desired, and they are compatible with incandescent lighting.

A recently developed light source that can be used as an alternative to fluorescent and incandescent lamps is the multivapor (metal halide) lamp. These lamps, being more compact sources than fluorescent lamps, can be used in fixtures similar to those used for incandescent lights. They have higher efficiencies than fluorescent and incandescent and also have good color rendering properties. They share the advantage of long life with fluorescent lamps. Fixtures using these lamps have some disadvantages for use in music rooms, however, such as their ballast noise and the fact that they are dimmable only at special expense. Therefore, they are not recommended for the typical auditorium or rehearsal room. Fluorescent lights also can have noisy ballasts and, even though dimming is possible at extra expense, they too must be used with special caution in these spaces. In some installations, it is feasible to locate the ballasts remotely to eliminate the noise problems inherent in fluorescent and multivapor fixtures.

Audience Areas

Lighting in the auditorium seating area need not be particularly bright unless the room also is used as a classroom. For reading programs at performances, 20 footcandles of dimmable light is required. For classroom use of the auditorium, 30 footcandles should be available. The source for classroom lighting can be a completely separate fixture system, either fluorescent or incandescent, with its own on-off switches located near the doors. For public performances, however, flexible control of the house lighting is very important, and a number of separate, dimmable circuits will be necessary to vary the area and quantity of light for different situations. Aisle and exit lights must not interfere with stage lighting effects.

Chippewa Hills High School, Remus, Michigan
Architects: Daverman Associates
Two separate lighting systems are used in this auditorium: dimmable incandescent lamps for performances, and fluorescent lights for classroom use.

Figure 6. Lighting Requirements for a Music/Drama Auditorium

Type of Lighting	Function	Controlled from	Fixtures/Instruments
House	Light audience area	Lighting control board	Incandescent only
Stage	Light performance area	Lighting control board	Floodlights, spotlights, scoops, special lights
Concert	Light performance area	Lighting control board	Downlights, floodlights
Work	Light rehearsal area with stage lights off	Wall switches, stage manager's control panel, lighting control board	General
Rehearsal	Light rehearsal area with stage lights off	Stage manager's control panel, lighting control board	Downlights, general lighting
Emergency	Permit audience and performers to escape building if power fails	Automatic switchover from house and stage circuits	May use some house lighting fixtures or separate floodlights
Panic	Provide immediate full light in the event of a panic in which building power does not fail	Stage manager's control panel, lighting control board	Uses existing systems
Aisle and Exit	Light steps and aisle and pin-point doors to provide safe egress from audience area when house is darkened	Lighting control board, panelboard	Special

---

Auditorium Lighting

Lighting the stage for performances can be as simple or as sophisticated as finances permit. A review of the projected uses for the auditorium produces a parallel list of lighting requirements for both the performing and audience areas. To these must be added the legal requirements for public safety. A complete lighting package that meets the needs of both dramatic and musical productions must be designed to meet the particular situation, since programing of activities and architectural considerations are different in every case. Lighting engineers trained and experienced in this special area are available to work as consultants to the design team and to advise the architect's lighting designers of the specifications to be laid out. Figure 6 provides a checklist of features that are included in a complete lighting system for a music/drama auditorium. Such a system requires the following components:

House lighting fixtures (some tied to emergency lighting, all tied to the panic lighting system)

Battery powered emergency lighting fixtures (if separate from above)

Aisle lighting fixtures

Exit lighting fixtures

Portable stage lighting fixtures

Stage lighting pipes or catwalks

Backstage performance lighting fixtures (running lights)

General backstage lighting fixtures (some tied to emergency, all to panic)

Rehearsal lighting fixtures

Load circuit plugging boxes

Load circuit plugging strips

Load circuit floor pockets

Interconnecting panel (can be omitted if a control circuit is provided for each load circuit)

Stage house lighting control console

Preset panel (if appropriate)

Memory bank (if appropriate)

Dimmer bank

Optional features to be considered if the auditorium is to be used by road shows are (1) a company switch, which enables traveling groups to wire their control board and operate lights through their own system; (2) an FOH transfer panel, which allows auditorium circuits for front of house lighting to be plugged into the traveling control system; and (3) remote stage and house lighting control stations, appropriately placed to enable one person to carry out all lighting control functions for films, simple concerts, and other auditorium activities.

COLOR

The selection of proper colors for all areas is an important detail in planning that often is neglected in the preoccupation with other phases of a building project. This is an element that costs little extra money and that often can save money in future maintenance if done carefully. Color selection is of particular importance in the music department because of the subtle interplay that exists between psychological and musical factors, especially in the rehearsal and performance of bands, orchestras, and choirs. The public, which supports the department by attendance at its events, also is sensitive to the effects of color on the performance-listening environment.

School auditoriums can be attractive places without expensive wood paneling or other costly decorative features. Intelligent choice of materials and use of color can do much to enhance the overall visual impression. Such a simple idea as varying the color of upholstery from seat to seat adds a visual interest that is eye-catching and yet adds little if anything to the cost. Whether selected by an interior decorator, a color consultant, a school committee (hopefully not), or the architect, colors should be based on a careful consideration of the following factors:

1. Color affects and influences people of all ages. Tests have shown that some colors stimulate and excite while others create fatigue, depression, and irritation.

2. Color plays an important part in creating an atmosphere

that promotes efficiency and morale among pupils and teachers alike.

3. Selecting colors that merely seem to be attractive may force those who occupy schoolrooms to work and study in surroundings that are psychologically unsuited to them. For example, abnormally high color contrasts have adverse effects. Such surroundings gradually may become irritating, affect work, and cause distress and unhappiness.

4. Elimination of these adverse conditions not only stimulates energy and improves concentration, but also raises morale. Color can help to bring about a better spirit of cooperation among teachers and students.

5. The correct use of color, combined with proper maintenance, gives teachers and students a feeling of pride in their surroundings and fosters a desire to keep them neat and orderly.

Warm and Cool

The blues and greens associated with the sky, lakes, and trees are cool colors. They frequently are recommended for rooms with western and southern exposures, which may feel overly warm from the sunshine. On the other hand, pale shades of yellow, orange, pink, and tan are warm colors. They frequently are recommended for classrooms with northern and eastern exposures. Cool, light pastels are receding colors that tend to make a room seem larger. The reverse generally is true of the warm colors. Greens, especially blue-greens, are quiet colors to which few people object.

Determining Values

Color value is important in two ways for schoolroom decoration. Lighter values should be used in rooms that tend to be dark, thus securing the maximum of reflected light. Lighter rooms may have darker walls. In rooms receiving strong glaring light, colors of medium or darker value reduce the strength of the reflected light. Color values can be used to equalize the distribution of reflected daylight in a room if selected and placed correctly. Light and dark color values can be used to change the apparent proportions of a long narrow room by painting the end walls in a relatively dark color, with a lighter value of that color or a harmonizing hue used on the long side walls. In juxtaposition to each other, dark colors seem to advance and light colors to retreat, making the length appear to diminish and the width increase. In square or nearly square rooms, the lack of interest in proportion often is made less apparent by painting one wall a hue different from that of the other three. The concentration of interest on one wall makes the sameness of dimension less noticeable. If the window wall is used for this purpose, it should be lighter than the others. If the opposite wall is used, it should be darker than the other three, in accordance with the rules of equalizing light.

Placement

Monotony throughout the school can be avoided by the choice and placement of colors. In classrooms, where it is important to secure and retain the attention of the pupils, color can help by providing a focal wall. The focal wall usually is painted a darker value of the color used on the other three walls or a contrasting color that will focus attention on that part of the

room. However, the color must not be conducive to eye strain. A slightly darker value usually is more restful than the lighter colors surrounding it.

The atmosphere in which teachers work should be an important consideration. They never should be forced to look into strong light. Wherever possible, a wall painted in a restful color should face the teacher. If a focal color is used on the front wall, the same color should be used on the opposite wall if the teacher faces it often. Because it comes from only one direction, the light in some classrooms seems particularly strong and concentrated on the wall opposite the window. The reflected light in such a room often is equalized by the use of wall colors in three values. The darkest color is applied to the wall opposite the windows where the light is strongest. The two end walls, which receive slightly less direct light, are painted in a lighter value, and the window wall, which receives little or no direct light, is painted the lightest value of the three.

In the average classroom, the ceiling should reflect the maximum amount of light. This restricts the range to white, off-white, or a very pale tint of a wall color or contrasting tint. Such colors should have reflection factors within the range of 80-85 percent.[10] In rooms where the maximum amount of light need not be reflected from the ceiling, a more pronounced color is not only effective from a decorative standpoint, but also may serve a functional purpose. In a room with a cold northern or eastern exposure, a ceiling in sunny yellow or light orange gives a cheerful effect. The glare of light from the west or south can be countered effectively by using light green or blue-green on the ceiling.

Selection

Color selection for auditoriums should take a number of variables into consideration: room volume and shape, carpets, drapes, seats, wall treatments, stage floor, light spill from projectors or other theatre lighting instruments, and stage drapes when used for masking or scenery. Areas that are to be invisible to the audience, such as the roof deck or upper side walls adjacent to a catwalk, must be painted flat black. Aside from these requirements, a small auditorium may use cool receding colors for vertical areas with the ceiling a contrasting warm hue. Larger auditoriums may use warm colors or a variety of warm and cool colors.

A music room may be treated as an area of some stimulation, employing warm and cool colors. Consideration should be given to the color of walls adjoining chalkboards, the color of the boards themselves, and the walls behind the conductor, all of which might be sources of eyestrain if too much contrast is present.

Offices should use light, both natural and artificial, for the eye comfort of the workers. Where the light is of higher intensity than required, colors having lower light reflection factors should be used. Where the light is adequate or slightly low, the color should have a higher light reflection factor. Where indirect lighting is used, the ceiling should be finished in white.

Rooms where the students occasionally are assembled should have an atmosphere as different as possible from their class-

---

[10]See color reflectance values inside the back cover of the I.E.S. *Lighting Handbook* (5th Edition).

rooms. The color background not only should be restful and relaxing in feeling, but also should put the student in the proper mental attitude to participate wholeheartedly in the activities of the assembly.

Relationship to the Lighting System

An important factor in the selection of colors is the original and *maintained* relationship with the lighting system. Lamps come in a wide variety of colors from the warm tones of incandescent to the various whites of fluorescent and metal halide lamps. The most commonly used to date have been the incandescent and the cool white fluorescent lamps. However, the improved color rendering properties of other sources, plus the increased availability of new fixture designs, have increased the use of a wide variety of light sources. The original intention of a color scheme in a room can be lost completely by changing types of lamps in the lighting system. Colored light affects colored paints in ways that often are unpredictable. Many times a room is repainted without regard to physical or psychological needs simply because there is leftover paint of a particular color or because a color can be obtained inexpensively. However, it is

important to keep a coordinated maintenance program of lighting and decorating that recognizes the two are not independent.

ELECTRICAL INSTALLATIONS

Many of the electrical considerations already have been discussed in the sections on the auditorium in Chapter 4 and in the earlier parts of this chapter. In addition to these, the installation of conduit for both audio and video cable should be included in the regular electrical contract. Since extra conduit is relatively inexpensive if installed during building construction, it makes good sense to provide extra conduit to each music room, connecting it to a central recording or control room. Lacking such a room it can be connected to a space adjacent to the school office. From here, closed-circuit or regular radio or television equipment may be installed and fed to a distribution system through this conduit. Where fluorescent lights are specified, they must have type A quiet ballasts that will not interfere with teaching or rehearsing in music rooms. Crucial areas, where recording may be done, should be lighted with incandescent fixtures that will not cause this noise problem. Electrical installations in lis-

University of Maryland
Architects: Henry Powell Hopkins & Associates
Extra conduit for both audio and video cables should be installed during building construction, when it is relatively inexpensive.

tening laboratories and electronic piano labs should be as safe-guarded as possible, with all electrical connections concealed and protected. The layout plans of such rooms should show where concealed conduit will be run. Access for servicing should be made as easy as possible.

AUDIO SYSTEMS

Sound Reinforcement

Although sound amplification seldom is used for musical performance, most auditoriums of over 200 to 300 seats have sound systems. Because this is an electronic age, audiences seem to expect amplification, at least for the spoken word. A good system, properly operated, is set at the lowest acceptable level and does not blare. In fact, the best sound amplification is undetectable. To accomplish this, the entire system must be of professional quality. If directionality of sound is to be retained, loudspeakers must be placed *above* the performing area, and never at the two sides. Portable or temporary systems seldom are satisfactory.

A point-source system with a single central loudspeaker cluster generally is recommended. Loudspeakers in the ceiling may be used when the auditorium ceiling is too low or sightlines are too poor to accommodate properly a central system.[11] Ceiling speaker systems, sometimes called distribution systems, often are inadequate because of four shortcomings:

1. The frequency response of the loudspeaker and its associated line-matching transformer are inadequate and thus unable to reproduce natural, full-range sound.

2. The typical small metal back-box restricts the low frequency response, and the usual baffle prevents smooth, even distribution of frequencies above 5,000 Hz.

3. Insufficient loudspeakers are provided for proper distribution. A realistic coverage angle for an eight-inch loudspeaker is 60 degrees, and it is considered good practice to provide 50 percent overlap at the listener's ear. A room with an 8- to 10-foot ceiling, for example, would require a large number of speakers.

4. Insufficient power is one of the most common failures in a distribution speaker system. It leads to distortion that includes loudspeaker overload as well as amplifier overload. This can be avoided by providing an amplifier and speaker system, both of which are used conservatively at one-tenth their rated capability.

If the above shortcomings are avoided carefully, a distributed speaker system can be effective. An additional precaution should be taken in large auditoriums with a long distance between the stage and the rear seats. Ceiling loudspeakers there may require a time-delay unit so that sound will not reach listeners in the back row over the loudspeakers before it arrives to them from the live source in the front of the room. Figure 7 shows the sound system requirements for multipurpose auditoriums.

In the usual system of bidding and awarding contracts for school buildings, the sound system frequently is listed as a part

[11]For a discussion of this subject, see Don Davis, "Analyzing Loudspeaker Locations for Sound Reinforcement Systems," *Journal of the Audio Engineering Society*, Vol. 17, No. 6 (December 1969).

Figure 7. Sound System Requirements for a Music/Drama Auditorium

System Function	Required for
Sound Reinforcement	Audience listening
Program Monitors	Control rooms, warm-up and dressing room, box office, lobby areas
Fold-back	Onstage performers of rock and amplified music
Recording	Later listening by performers; possible radio or disc use
Sound Effects	Dramatic productions
Playback	Playing the discs or tapes into the audience chamber
Audience Recall and Paging	Signalling end of intermission (may be played through program monitors if no separate bell system is used)

---

of the electrical contract, with the winning electrical firm subcontracting the system in turn to his lowest bidder. Since school contracts seldom include performance specifications for the sound system, this is one place where the contractor can cut corners. To guarantee a good sound reinforcement system, the design should be made by a competent sound engineer. The engineer must get adequate information from the future user and then draw up specifications that will include equipment by brand name and number. If at all possible, the sound system should be separate from the electrical contract, and made an independent agreement between the school and the sound system contractor. The work should be reviewed and tested by the sound engineer to be certain it meets specifications before it is accepted.

The control position for an auditorium sound system must be placed within the audience chamber itself where the operator hears the direct sound as the audience hears it. Locating it in a control room where the signal is processed through mixers, amplifiers, and speakers is too unreliable for effective and subtle sound control. Microphones must be placed near the source of sounds being picked up and must be arranged carefully to give good balance if more than one source is amplified. For operatic and theater performances, a number of microphones can be placed in the footlights, with proper resilient mounting to avoid thumping sounds from people walking on stage. The operator in the control booth must follow the performance and keep live only those microphones that are near the sources being amplified. For orchestral or choir pickup, additional microphones are needed overhead, and the relative operating levels must be adjusted by experiment. Most musicians have a rather strong prejudice against amplification. However, high-quality professional-grade equipment, operated skillfully, can enhance the quality of many musical performances. This is especially true in large convention halls or gymnasiums where musical performances sometimes are given, and outdoors where the background sound level is not very low. The design of each sound system should not be left to suppliers of equipment.

Calvin College, Grand Rapids, Michigan
Architects: Daverman Associates and The Perkins & Will Partnership
Acoustics: Russell Johnson
The booth for recording and broadcasting should be located at the rear of the auditorium, adjacent to lighting control.

Recording and Broadcasting

Recent improvements in recording equipment and televised education have led many schools to incorporate facilities for these new techniques. Space should be allowed both for receiving and for broadcasting music. The control booth should be well insulated for sound and should have slanted double glass windows for viewing the performing groups. Such a control booth sometimes is located either adjacent to the auditorium stage or between rehearsal halls. The ideal location, however, is at the rear of the auditorium, adjacent to lighting control, sound effects, sound reinforcement, and other systems. Integration, or at least juxtaposition, of these control areas makes possible more efficient operation, which is particularly important when several systems are used simultaneously, such as for musical theater or operetta performance.

The control booth is the electronic nerve-center of the building, and conduit for audio and video cables should connect it to every music classroom, rehearsal room, and teaching studio, as well as to various locations in the auditorium. Easy access to the rooftop for antenna connections and to the basement for cable runs in open troughs (which are much less expensive than conduit and just as good for audio-video cables) also should be provided. The size and layout of the recording-sound-control booth often is compromised in order to gain a desirable location. Such

accommodation to space, however, should not penalize present or future programs. The assistance of a trained sound engineer will help to produce the best room design for efficient use. The equipment to be installed will have an effect on room layout and size.

Music Playback

Provision for music playback in the auditorium, rehearsal rooms, music classrooms, and perhaps other rooms should be included in the planning stage. Such matters as placement of wall-mounted loudspeakers, for example, need to be determined so that concealed conduit for speaker cables can be installed. Electrical outlets must be placed strategically. In many cases, the local playback system can be fed from the recording booth. Equipment for music playback must be compatible with the primary systems in the control booth. It must be of good quality, high fidelity, and preferably designed into the space where it is to be used—not added after the fact. It should be versatile and accommodate various modes.

Electronic Music

Complete music facilities often include a specially-equipped studio for the composition of electronic music. Low-cost equipment for this purpose increasingly is available. Many state universities have electronic music studios staffed by people competent to advise on the type of space and equipment required. Equipment will include synthesizers, tone generators, tape recorders (preferably with variable speed control), filters, mixers, amplifiers, reverberation devices, time-delay units, duplicating facilities, and monitor loudspeakers. Adequate sturdy shelving to house the equipment, concealed conduit or cable troughs, and a convenient workbench and tape-editing facility should be provided, as well as ample storage space for tapes and records.

House Intercommunication

Every auditorium should be provided with proper equipment for interhouse communication. The number of stations and their locations will depend on the programing plans for the facility, but a useful checklist of positions to be considered is the following:

1. Light control booth
2. Sound effects position
3. Recording booth
4. Projection location
5. Stage left
6. Stage right
7. Conductor's position, orchestra lift
8. Lighting catwalks
9. Manager's office
10. Box office
11. Dressing rooms
12. Drama director's position: row 10 or 11 in the auditorium (a removable phone plugs into a floor outlet)
13. Drama director's position: rear-auditorium control booth.

For more elaborate productions, a stage manager's desk and panel with provision for communicating with performers and other technicians is very useful; it is nearly indispensable for Broadway-type shows. The auditorium communication system can be tied into the central school system if desired. In this case, special precautions must be taken to prevent feeding announce-

University of Maryland
Architects: Henry Powell Hopkins & Associates
Music departments are making increased use of closed-circuit television.

ments or broadcasts into the auditorium during public performances.

Sound Effects

The music director rarely, if ever, has occasion to call upon a sound effects system. But a drama coach sharing an auditorium with the music department would find it hard to accept a hall without one. In its simplest form, it should provide for playing tapes through an amplifier and switching system that will feed audio signals to a number of locations at the sides, rear, or above the stage. These lines terminate in audio receptacles that can accept plugs for portable loudspeakers.

VISUAL SYSTEMS

Scenery Projection

Open stages and modified proscenium stages frequently use projected backgrounds. When delivered from a catwalk or ceiling slot above the stage, optical correction makes possible a rather steep angle that permits actors to come within five feet of the image without blocking the light path. Best results are obtained when the screen is permanent—preferably plaster on a wall—and thus not subject to unevenness or to movement from drafts on stage, both of which faults will distort the image and destroy its effectiveness. The screen is not beaded in order to avoid reflecting stage lighting to the audience. Rear projection is another system that can be used for scenery and other theatrical effects. It is especially effective for television. It requires space behind a translucent rather than opaque screen.

Slides and Movies

State and local fire codes restrict the kinds of movie projectors that can be used in an open auditorium or in a projection room that is not enclosed completely and equipped with a sprinkler system. The 16mm movie projectors meet these requirements and can be equipped with long-throw lenses to make projection from a rear booth practical. Since movie machines are noisy, they should be confined to an isolated booth. When this is not possible, portable enclosures on casters can be devised for in-house movie projection. In either case, provision must be made for plugging into the house sound system, with remote volume control at the operator's position. If movie projection is from a booth, a monitor loudspeaker must be provided and equipped with its own volume control. A remote house-lighting dinner

within easy reach of the projectionist will make possible one-man operation of house lighting, movie sound, and picture.

Slide projectors that can throw a bright picture from the rear of an auditorium are very costly, so slides usually must be shown from a much closer position. The noise of the blower can be very distracting when it is placed within range of the audience. Provision for remote operation will allow a lecturer to advance his own slides from his stage position. Placement of the projection screen is a consideration if it is to be permanently mounted. It must be at the proper height to avoid keystoning, and it must not interfere with stage lighting or other accouterments.

Television

The development of public television for educational purposes, and the perfection of video-recording and closed-circuit television systems, makes planning for use of these tools important. This can be integrated into plans for audio recording and radio reception. The decision to incorporate television in a school probably will not be made to fulfill the needs of the music department alone. Nevertheless, there are certain uses of this teaching tool that music educators should consider in planning for the future.[12] Closed circuit television is used increasingly to provide general education experiences in music for the whole student body. Conduits from the stage and sound control room to selected positions throughout the school will enable such use. If a complete system is considered too costly now, the conduit should be installed in the building at the time of construction, when its cost is relatively low. The auditorium also should be equipped for large group viewing. Television monitoring systems may be helpful in some practice rooms. Informal instrumental instruction sometimes is given over educational television, and schools may want to provide the means of receiving these lessons in the music department. The portable videotape recorder is a tool of great potential value to music educators. The video cassette and video disc are recent developments that offer additional possibilities.

Special Effects

Special effects can be either visual or aural. Black lights or strobe lights use floor outlets in the front of the stage controlled from the lighting booth. Full surround sound or rotating sound easily are possible if conduit to six or eight loudspeaker positions is located around the perimeter of the audience seating area.

[12]See Thomas H. Carpenter, *Televised Instruction in Music* (Washington, D. C.: Music Educators National Conference, 1973).

Chapter 6: Equipment

A music department that is poorly equipped cannot progress at the desired rate no matter how excellently it is housed. In far too many schools, able directors are seriously handicapped by the lack of proper equipment. An important maxim in purchasing any school equipment is *buy something good and then take care of it*. Modern furniture and equipment should be reviewed right up to move-in-day. Educational development tends to precede design of the new equipment that answers its requirements. Do not furnish a 1975 or 1980 facility with 1950 equipment.

INSTRUMENTS

Pianos

Upright pianos can be used in music rooms, but for major musical activities, a grand piano should be available. It is always advisable to purchase the largest possible piano for the location and budget. Tone quality depends on the size of the sounding board area and the length of strings for the lower tones. The keyboard height and pedal height should be standardized to that of the large grand pianos. Many manufacturers are incorporating plastics into piano manufacture. Plastic key covering has proved satisfactory and perhaps even superior to ivory. Plastic action parts, and particularly plastic bushings, have not proved to be satisfactory. For school pianos, good

wooden action parts and felt bushings still give the best service. Upright pianos that are to be moved should be mounted on large rubber ball-bearing casters, or on piano gliders equipped with this type of caster. Grand pianos should be mounted on a glider that does not raise the piano so high that operation of the pedals is difficult.

It is not advisable to purchase inexpensive pianos because of their heavy daily use and long period of expected service. A poorly constructed piano cannot produce desirable tone quality, often does not hold its tuning, and is not dependable mechanically. Each school, with the aid of staff and consultants, can make its own specifications for pianos when requesting bids. In preparing such specifications, consideration should be given to the following items: overall size, cabinet and finish, casters, key bed, keys, plate, back and pin plank, tuning pins, sounding board, ribs, bridges, action, and musical tone. In addition, special conditions and factors may indicate the need for keyboard cover locks, special sized racks, dust covers, or other items. All pianos should be tuned to A-440 three or four times a year. It is unfair to ask students to listen to or perform on a piano when an appreciable adjustment of tuning is required.

Electronic pianos are finding increasing favor with schools and colleges for class piano instruction and theory classes. The expense of a system with six electronic pianos is less than the cost of a grand piano. Their use is discussed in Chapter 3, page 20.

Organs

Several decisions must be made on the basis of the music department's objectives and, to some extent, the educational level of the students using the facilities: (1) whether an organ will be installed in a recital hall, (2) if there will be a teaching studio or practice room equipped with an organ, or (3) if the organ will be electronic or pipe. The planner should not purchase an electronic instrument without investigating the possibility of a small pipe organ, at least in the recital hall or auditorium. Whenever possible, students should be educated on authentic instruments. In some situations, however, the electronic organ represents the only alternative. In this case, an electronic organ should be selected with stops and voicing that parallel the traditional pipe organ as closely as possible.

Band and Orchestra Instruments

Certain musical instruments that are necessary for every band or orchestra should be provided by the institution, especially those that generally are not suitable for solo playing, are expensive, are not popular, or are difficult to transport. These instruments may include string bass, tuba, timpani, bassoon, harp, celesta, English horn, alto clarinet, bass clarinet, contrabass clarinet, bass drum, baritone saxophone, bass saxophone, chimes, vibraphone, xylophone, marimba, contrabassoon, concert snare drum, field snare drum, flugelhorn, and percussion traps. In addition, some schools may include D trumpet, A clarinet, horn, oboe, violoncello, viola, euphonium, and bass trombone.

In some systems, the school owns some or all of the various band and orchestra instruments. These instruments are loaned or rented to the students for trial periods in order to get large numbers of students started on musical instruments. This plan often is begun in elementary school and carried over to junior and senior high school. Because there are certain problems in scheduling many different kinds of instruments, and because the basis for the instrumentation depends mainly on the violin, cornet, and clarinet, these instruments should be supplied in relatively large numbers and put in the elementary schools. Many school systems furnish the following instruments in the elementary schools:

Violin: quarter, half, and full size
Viola: for the larger students, some schools use full-size violins strung as violas in order to teach the alto clef
Violoncello: quarter, half, and full size
String bass: quarter, half, and full size
Oboe: with simplified system of fingering
B-flat clarinet
Horn: double and single
Cornet
Trombone
Baritone
Tuba: small upright E-flat tuba
Full percussion equipment

High schools and colleges should provide instruments required for complete instrumentation, such as piccolo, A clarinet, English horn, bassoon, bass trombone, and CC tuba for orchestra: alto clarinet, bass clarinet, contrabass clarinet, and upright BB flat tuba for concert band work; and parade drums and sousaphone for marching band.

AUDIOVISUAL EQUIPMENT

Fully equipping a new music facility with audiovisual equipment can involve considerable funds, to which must be added the costs of stocking magnetic tape, transparencies, and films each year. Maintenance and repair of equipment also must be budgeted. Careful consideration should be taken in advance to be certain that the equipment will be used with some regularity by the music teacher.

Tape Recording

Tape recorders allow the student to record his own playing, listen to the performance of a professional, or have a permanent record made of a reading session of his original manuscript. Lessons in theory, harmony, and music history can be pre-recorded, used at the student's convenience, and repeated as often as desired. Recordings of performances can be used to improve interpretation, tone quality, balance, and technique. Most units sold today are not of adequate quality to satisfy the needs of the serious music student. Poor equipment will defeat the purpose for which it is used. *Only equipment of professional quality should be considered by schools, since theirs is a professional use in every sense of the word.* The music educator should avoid the consumer-oriented shops, and rather should contact a professional audio dealer for advice, selection, and installation of equipment. If an audio consultant is retained to design the auditorium sound system, he can be used to draw up specifications for the recording and listening equipment for the rest of the building. Specifications presented in this section should be considered as minimum, since future equipment undoubtedly will be better.

Magnetic Tape

A tape system consists of two elements: the magnetic tape, and its transport with the associated electronics. Both are fundamental parts of the system, and a compromise on either will produce inferior results. This is true of both reel-to-reel and cassette recorders. Standard brand-name tape is best in the long run. White box tape often is sold with a private brand name at a reduced price. Such tape must be avoided, since it often was made for other purposes originally, such as substandard computer tape, and may deposit excessive oxide on tape heads and drive units, or be unlubricated or excessively abrasive.

Tape is supplied on 5-, 7-, and 10-inch reels. Smaller reels than these are not practical for high quality machines. Length of tape on the reel is determined both by its diameter and by the thickness of the tape. Tapes less than 1 mil thick should be avoided, with 1½ mil tapes being standard. A 7-inch reel of the former yields 45 minutes of recording time at 7½ ips or 90 minutes at 3¾ ips; 1½ mil tapes give 30 minutes at 7½ ips or 60 minutes at 3¾ ips. The thinner tapes not only are difficult to handle and prone to breakage, but also are poor for storage and tend to aggravate print-through and other problems. If the tape is to be used only for study purposes, a good general purpose tape is sufficient. If, however, the recording will be used to make

Only professional quality recording equipment should be considered by educational facilities.

photograph records, it should be made on low-noise tape. Assignments for listening centers using student-operated equipment should be recorded on extra-strength tapes that will resist wear and breakage. Mylar-based tapes may stretch if subjected to hard handling or if used on a machine that is out of adjustment; stretching renders a tape unusable. It is better to have a tape break, which is a characteristic of acetate-based tapes, than to have it stretch, since breaks readily are spliced and the tape then can continue to be used.

For many years, magnetic tapes were made of fine particles of iron oxide adhered to an acetate or mylar base. New formulas recently have been developed, especially for cassette tapes, that use chromium oxide to improve the recording characteristics available at slower speeds. Other new coatings are in the experimental stage. Blank cassettes offer fewer options than reel-to-reel tape, but also are available in different thicknesses and lengths. The 30-minute cassette tape (in one direction) is standard.

Reel-to-Reel Recorders

A wide range of so-called professional tape recorders is available. Unfortunately, the word "professional" has been misused, and the prospective buyer should be wary of misleading representation. Even published specifications should be viewed with

some scepticism, since some important element often is left out. A reliable dealer can demonstrate the equipment and point out various features. In general, the faster the tape speed the better the fidelity. Machines today can record at 7½ ips with a fidelity achieved only at 15 or 30 ips ten years ago. Even 3¾ ips on certain machines is now acceptable for all but the most critical uses. A reel capacity of 7 inches is adequate, although 10-inch reels offer twice the uninterrupted recording time. Frequency response should be flat ± 2 decibels from 30-15,000 Hz, with a signal-to-noise ratio of 60 decibels and flutter and wow measurements not over 0.15.

Tape recorders have great practicality because they are easy to operate, transport, and store. Sensible use keeps maintenance costs to a minimum. Preventive maintenance must be exercised at recommended intervals, and tape heads and drive mechanism must be kept scrupulously clean. Tape machines with internal amplifiers and loudspeakers are not satisfactory for music department use. A separate tape deck, amplifier, and loudspeakers are required, particularly if stereophonic or four-channel tapes are used. Since monophonic, stereophonic, and quadraphonic systems are available, the choice is left to the user. Stereophonic systems presently provide the greatest fidelity and versatility. Four-channel sound is developing rapidly and will find future applications in large educational institutions.

At one time, full-track monaural recordings using the complete quarter-inch width of the tape were considered necessary for excellent quality reproduction. With the advent of stereo, two channels were recorded simultaneously, each using half the tape width. For four-channel sound or the narrow tape widths required by small cassettes, very narrow recordings tracks still are producing excellent fidelity with good signal-to-noise ratio. This is due in part to the development of noise reduction systems, such as the Dolby, which should be included in the electronics of any narrow-track open reel or cassette recorder.

Cassette Recorders

Open reel tape recorders, with their faster speeds, wider tape, and larger reel capacity, will continue to set standards in the future. For educational purposes, however, the cassette player has great potential. Improved drive mechanisms, better tapes, noise-reduction systems, and the convenience of portability all are important factors. Units are available that, when played through an external amplifier and speaker system, can equal or exceed the quality of disc recordings. Quality cassette recorders can meet specifications that once were reserved for professional open reel machines.

Listening Centers

The music listening center parallels the foreign language laboratory in offering new approaches to education. Programmed materials that allow self-instruction in ear training readily are available on tape. Student practice can be monitored for later evaluation by the student himself or the instructor. Selections can be taped for students in music history and appreciation classes. Listening centers can be as simple or as complex as the available space and money allow, since usually they are custom-designed for the particular installation. These are discussed in Chapter 3, pages 20-22.

Record Players

Phonograph records have advantages over tapes and cassettes for certain educational uses. They are more easily handled for class use, since the instructor can skip selections more easily than with tape. Records are disadvantageous from the standpoint of wear and distortion. Even with proper care, the quality of a heavily used record will deteriorate. Two basic types of record players are available: the turntable and the record changer. Better reproduction generally is available from the simple turntable assembly, and the instructor can locate a specific spot on a recording more quickly. Record changers, however, have some advantages and often lower cost. Their automatic features can help reduce scratches and record wear caused by manual placing of the tone arm. In recent years, record changers have improved in quality so that many models are able to meet the exacting criteria formerly met only by a turntable unit. On either type of machine, a cuing level for the tone arm is especially useful. Diamond styluses are the only practical kind for school use. When used carefully in a tone arm with light tracking force, they can withstand many weeks of frequent use. A stylus microscope to check for wear is a worthwhile accessory. Replacement styluses always should be made by the manufacturer of the cartridge.

FM Radio

A large number of high fidelity educational radio stations now broadcast throughout the United States, usually featuring many hours of serious music programing each day. In some large metropolitan areas, there are also commercial FM stations using similar programs. With the conversion to stereo by most of these stations, the material they broadcast has become even more desirable for educational uses. The possibility of tape recording broadcasts for use at a more convenient time also is an appealing feature. However, this can be done legally only by first securing permission from the copyright holder. Most stations can provide a list of scheduled performances several weeks in advance to facilitate this process. Addition of an FM radio tuner to the recording or playback system requires a very modest investment in terms of its potential value to the school music program, since it can use existing amplifier and speakers. The desirability of a recording-broadcasting control booth is discussed in Chapter 3. This booth is the ideal location for an FM tuner if it is not located in the school office as part of the master intercommunication system. From the sound control booth, programs can be broadcast to the school system.

Classroom Playback Systems

Playback systems for music classrooms, rehearsal rooms, or teaching studios should be designed with careful consideration of their planned use. With the many options available using discs, tapes, and cassettes, a system can become too complex for convenient use. Mounting the players and controls in a portable cabinet on casters can make the system readily accessible. A self-coiling cord carrying audio and electrical connections is helpful. Classroom playback systems should have both disc and reel-to-reel tape capabilities. Tape decks without recording amplifiers are adequate for these rooms. Systems should have stereophonic electronics, and the loudspeakers ideally should be wall-mounted with concealed wiring and spaced 8-10 feet apart, depending on the size of the room. Four-channel capabilities should be kept in mind, so that forthcoming developments in multichannel systems do not make the equipment obsolete.

Tape recording capabilities for rehearsal rooms and private teaching studios allow rehearsals and lessons to be taped and reviewed by teacher and pupils. All the audio components in each system must be compatible and of relatively equal quality. One low-quality component will reduce the effect of all other components. A professional audio engineer can offer wise counsel on matching the units of the system and installing cassette players or radio tuners as well as the basic disc and tape players. The system should have enough power-handling capacity to serve the room in which it is located.

Auditorium Playback Systems

Auditorium playback systems should be independent of the sound reinforcement system but at least equal in quality to it. The reasons for this are that the sound amplification system usually is controlled from the rear of the auditorium, where it is not accessible to someone teaching or playing records on stage or at the front of the hall, and that the sound system usually is monaural. For maximum flexibility, the auditorium playback system should be movable, with the component cabinet and

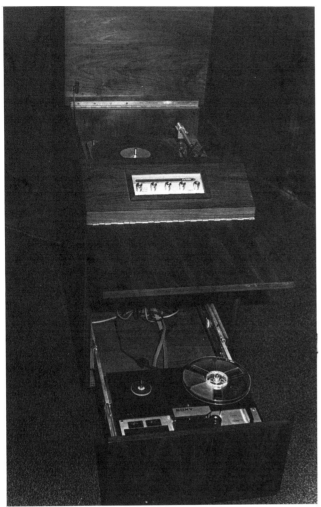

Players and controls can be mounted in a portable cabinet on casters.

loudspeakers each mounted on large casters. Stereophonic disc, tape, and cassette units should be incorporated into this system, with enough power to fill the entire hall at high level if necessary. This does not exclude the possibility of playing tapes or discs through the auditorium sound system.

Central Sound Systems

The equipment by which radio programs and announcements are distributed throughout the school usually is shared by the entire building and therefore is only partially the responsibility of the music department. Most systems are equipped so that classrooms can be monitored from the central switchboard, and the equipment used as a two-way communication system between the classroom and office. All equipment should be purchased from a well-established manufacturer and installed by engineers experienced in such work. Even so, the best of these systems is suitable only for carrying spoken announcements or background music, and the music teacher should resist attempts to use this system for serious music reproduction. The small speakers that are satisfactory for spoken announcements are inadequate for musical reproduction.

Portable Public Address Systems

Portable systems usually are shared with other departments. Since this equipment may be used for outdoor band concerts and musical performances in auditoriums not permanently equipped, the same supervision should be exercised in its selection as for the central system. Microphones should be high quality cardioid, and the amplifiers should have sufficient reserve power to reproduce music without distortion. A fifty-watt amplifier is the absolute minimum for use outdoors and in large auditoriums. High quality speakers mounted in bass-reflex baffles generally are most satisfactory for musical purposes provided that extreme volume is unnecessary and that problems of microphone placement do not accentuate their tendency to feedback. In conditions involving these difficulties, horn-type speakers may be necessary, but they must be selected with great care because many horn-type speakers have poor fidelity characteristics. The light, self-contained, battery-powered megaphone is of considerable use in drilling the marching band. It is of no use for musical amplification, but its extreme portability and ease of operation make it a valuable rehearsal aid.

Monitoring Systems

Where a number of practice rooms are used at one time, the teacher should be able to supervise them all from his office. This is accomplished by an inexpensive intercommunications system that has a switchboard installed in the director's office. Since it will be used primarily for casual inspection, a system using a compact loudspeaker that can be reversed and used as a microphone is adequate. A number of variations in application can be suggested by the engineers supplying such equipment.

Tuning Devices

The standard tuning bar for instrumental rooms has given way to its electronic counterpart. The electronic tuner has the advantages of added volume, variable pitch, and continuous sound. Transistorized, battery-operated models free the tuner from the electrical cord and require no warm-up time. Some models incorporate a convenient metronome. Tuning stroboscopes, both chromatic and single pitch, are available for school use and are helpful in teaching and checking intonation. A visual indication of pitch is given, and the student can see when he is in tune. Its greatest potential value to the instrumental department is for personal work in overcoming intonation problems on an individual instrument. It should not be used as a substitute for eartraining and tuning by ear in full rehearsal. The device may have other uses in the music and physics departments. Other electronic instruments have been developed to train students in judging intonation. Some can reproduce the entire chromatic scale in one or more octaves. Others are keyboard operated and permit adjustment of various intervals and tuning to just or tempered scales. Another electronic device visualizes volume levels.

Metronomes

In addition to spring-driven, pendulum-type metronomes, there also are many electric metronomes available. Different pulsations are obtained easily and accurately by simple adjustment of a dial. In addition to the aural indication, some have a

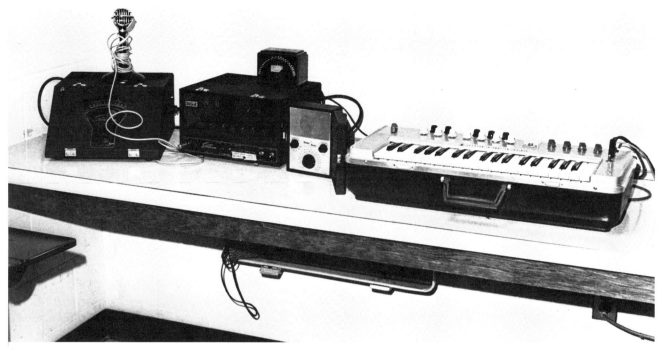

Several varieties of electronic tuning instruments are available.

small blinking light. If there is a large volume of sound, such as in drum practice, this visual indication is of considerable value. There are also metronomes that will produce multiple beat patterns simultaneously. A pocketwatch sized wind-up metronome or transistorized miniature unit are useful for checking tempos of processionals or marching bands.

Other Electronic Equipment

Numerous other electronic devices are available for a variety of specialized uses. Portable classroom organs, electronic music blackboards, teaching machines, and punch-tape controlled electronic programers are examples of some that may be useful in special situations.

Projectors

Whether a part of the music department equipment or made available through the audiovisual department, a good 16mm sound projector is essential. Many excellent music films are available. The equipment should have the capability of being played through quality listening equipment in the room.

Projectors for 2-inch slides and for filmstrips are available separately and in combination. For school purposes, the combination units may be the most desirable. Lantern slide projectors (3½ inches by 4 inches) are available in modern design. The ease with which slide materials can be prepared for this device make it attractive. The advantages of the overhead projector have made it a widely used piece of equipment in recent years. With special equipment, transparencies can be made by photocopy process. Opaque projectors, though much improved, still require a darkened room. Improved models now can project a sheet of music up to 8½"×11".

Screens

Certain rooms in the music suite should be provided with wall or ceiling-mounted screens, with portable screens available for other locations. The size and shape of the screens is determined by room size and audience capacity as well as the type of projector. In planning the location of the screen, it should be remembered that the beam of light must strike the screen at a 90-degree angle to avoid distortion. Enough space must be allowed at the front of the room so that no pupil is less than two screen widths away. If the auditorium has a proscenium arch, it should be high enough to accommodate a screen whose width is approximately one-sixth the depth of the audience area. Controls for raising and lowering auditorium screens should be provided in the projection areas as well as backstage.

Duplicating Equipment

The music department in a large school may not find it satisfactory to rely on the duplicating equipment that serves the entire school. Because of new copying methods, the old spirit duplicator is considered obsolete in some schools. However, it does provide fast, inexpensive, purple copies for class use. The mimeograph is still a mainstay in providing inexpensive and relatively attractive programs, black and white copies of instructions or activities calendars, handbooks, and many of the day-to-day needs of a music program. An offset press or multilith is a possibility for large departments, but usually is limited to purchase by the entire school system rather than a single department. The ubiquitous photocopy machine has revolutionized the entire field of copying and duplicating, and is hard to match in speed and convenience. Copyright violations through the use of this machine have been widespread, and the Music Educators National Conference has taken a firm stand in cautioning its membership to avoid any illegal copying of copyrighted music scores or other material.

FURNITURE AND OTHER EQUIPMENT

Music Stands

Schools should purchase high quality nonfolding stands that are durable—telescopic metal stands with nonbreakable bases. The number of stands for an instrumental group can be estimated at a ratio of 1 : 1½. Extra stands are needed for the prac-

tice rooms. Students often provide their own folding music stands for special appearances when school stands cannot be transported easily.

Chairs and Chairstands

High quality *nonfolding* chairs are recommended for music seats. Comfort should be a major consideration, but the chairs must encourage students to sit erect. Chair legs should have rubber tips or rounded metal plates to protect the floors. A shelf under each chair can store books and music unless some other provision is made for these. Chairs for singers should provide back support. Cellists should have chairs that permit them to sit on the forward edge. Posture chairs designed for music rooms always are preferable to regular seating. These are available with drop or removable tablet arms if the rehearsal room doubles as a classroom.

String bass players should have stools approximately 30 inches high or adjustable metal chair stands that include footrests and adjustable pin cups. Similar specially designed chair stands for tuba and sousaphone help hold the heavy and cumbersome instrument in correct playing position and provide convenient and safe storage. A swivel stool with adjustable height is desirable for the tympanist.

COURTESY WENGER CORPORATION

Left and lower left: Special chairstands can be used to hold heavy or cumbersome instruments, such as these for Sousaphone and string bass.

Lower right: A podium chairstand allows the conductor to sit or stand during rehearsals.

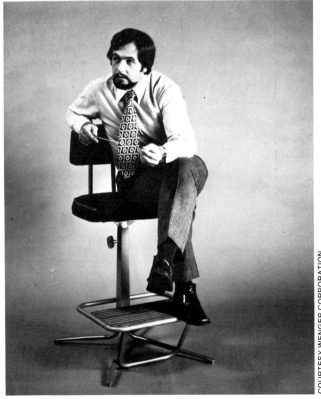

COURTESY WENGER CORPORATION

Conductor's Podium

The podium should be movable and constructed to match the room or stage. The minimum size is approximately 8 inches high and 2½-3 feet square. For large choral or instrumental groups, a two-step podium, 16 inches high with an 8-inch step on each side, may be desirable. For safety, the top should be covered with corrugated vinyl tread or, for greater comfort, a piece of rubber-backed carpeting. Metal gliders placed on the corners will prevent scratching the floor. Large podiums should be provided with cut-outs or handles for easy carrying. Factory-made podiums are available in either folding or fixed units.

Many school conductors favor the approach of most professionals and prefer to be seated during rehearsals, particularly with small ensembles. A podium chair stand has an adjustable padded swivel seat and a built-in podium that permits standing to conduct as well. An oversized music rack is useful, and this can be combined with a folio storage cabinet or even tape and record-playing equipment if desired.

Risers

Risers of various kinds are an important part of the equipment for any music department. The merits of built-in or movable risers in rehearsal rooms is discussed in Chapter 3. If risers will be built in, in spite of the strictures their use places on an instrumental room, their width and location are critical. Too great a width wastes space and spreads out the performers much more than they will be on a flat stage floor. If the school has no orchestra, riser widths smaller than 60 inches work well; 48 inches is adequate for a single row of instrumentalists playing wind instruments. Space requirements for a row of flutes or clarinets, for example, are much different from those for a row of cellos or bass viols. The top riser should be up to 120 inches wide since the back of the room ordinarily accommodates the larger percussion and bass instruments. If storage cabinets in the rear of the room have swinging doors, adequate room should be left so they can be opened when the top riser is occupied. A height of 6 or 8 inches per step is adequate to provide good sightlines. The number of terraces ranges from three to five depending on the size of the room and the organizations using it. Risers should be kept as far back in the room as possible so that there is plenty of space in front for the sound to mix. This also provides a convenient flat floor area where chamber ensembles can meet.

If portable risers are moved between rehearsal room and auditorium stage, ease of folding and moving are paramount considerations. Factory-made risers incorporate special hardware and strong metals in ways usually not possible if manufactured in a school shop. Lightweight aluminum is incorporated into many ready-made units to combine strength with lightness and easy maneuverability. Two sets of risers, one to be kept in the auditorium and another for the rehearsal hall, avoid some of the logistical problems. However, many directors find the flat floor of the stage satisfactory even if risers are used in the rehearsal room. Many professional symphony orchestras have abandoned the use of risers because elevated brass and percussion sections almost always overbalance the strings. This may be even more true for school orchestras. However, the visual aspects may override other considerations.

These reinforced portable risers and stage fit on their own castered storage truck.

Risers are available for standing chorus, seated chorus, or band and orchestra. Dimensions and capacities are readily available in suppliers' and manufacturers' catalogs. Units are available in rectangular or wedge-shaped sections to fit the dimensions of any room or stage. While risers can be built by school industrial arts or carpentry shops, such construction is no longer as popular as it once was. Because of liability laws, manufacturers are not able to make their own special hardware available separately, since the proper use and assembly of this hardware is an important part of its safety. Homemade units tend to be heavy and cumbersome and take more room to store. If the risers are to be shop-built in the school in spite of these disadvantages, the catalogs should be consulted for established dimensions and riser heights. The school board must accept the legal responsibility that goes with product manufacture.

Bulletin and Chalk Boards

The corkboard for official notices should be near the music director's office, built into the wall. It can be encased in glass with an inside light and equipped with a locking door. Another board can be reserved for posting general notices, advertisements, cartoons, and other information. A minimum size for the bulletin board is 30 inches by 30 inches.

Chalkboards, at least some of which should be permanent fixtures, are needed in rehearsal areas to list rehearsal schedules, emphasize important announcements, or serve as general teaching aids. Portable chalkboards with one slate side and one cork side have many uses in a music department. Light green chalkboards are recommended. Some chalkboards should have staff lines on them approximately 1 inch apart with 3 or 4 inches between staves. Some manufacturers will line the boards at the factory.

Sorting Racks

A music sorting rack can be used equally well by both vocal and instrumental organizations. Such a rack is convenient for distributing music to folders and for reassembling the music when ready for storage again. A sorting rack should consist of four to five slanting shelves, 1 inch by 15 inches by 75 inches, with 1 inch by 2 inch strips at the bottom of each shelf to hold the music in place. Each shelf of the sorting rack should be able to hold a desired number of these folders, allowing 2 inches between folios. Two or more racks placed against the corner walls of the music library, rehearsal room, or office make it possible to use the racks with a minimum of walking. Sufficient shelf space should be provided for the greatest number of folios used by any one musical organization.

Storage Cabinets

The location of storage rooms is discussed in Chapter 3. Providing a separate space large enough to store all the instruments so the players can get at them easily is not always practical. Some locked storage around the periphery of the rehearsal room plus a separate, well organized instrument room makes a good combination in many situations. Additional rehearsal room floor should be added to allow for the space occupied by the cabinets and a passageway in front of them. This can add 200 to 500 square feet to the dimensions of a rehearsal room.

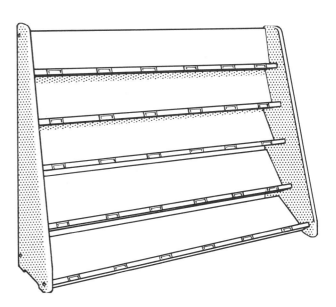

Above: A sorting rack is convenient for distributing and reassembling music.

Below: Instrument storage lockers are available with compartments to accommodate instruments of different sizes.

Left: An attractive castered, locking percussion cabinet can be used for both storage and performance

Below: The repair bench should have a sink with running water, gas unit, electrical outlets, and storage space, as well as convenient work surfaces.

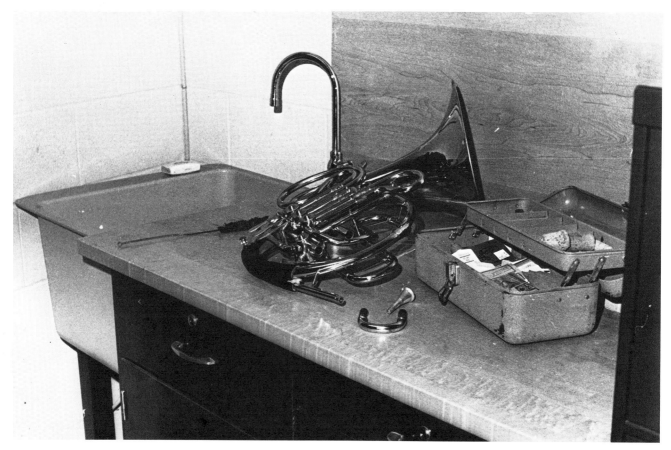

Cabinetry placed in storage areas should be designed for the most efficient use of the space, provide convenient access for the user, and be safe and secure. Shelves should be large enough to accept stored items readily but not so large that they waste space. Uncased instruments should lie on carpeted shelves to protect them from denting or scratching. Cabinets should be open to air movement so that ventilation and humidity can be kept constant.

Provision should be made for both day-to-day storage and more permanent storage in a locked closet. A recent study revealed that most thievery of school and privately owned instruments is by school employees and students. Some protection is provided by individual instrument lockers equipped with padlocks. Security has become an overriding consideration in some schools, and this aspect of the storage problem should not be minimized.

With increasing school use of amplified instruments, many music storage areas built to accommodate only traditional instruments are inadequate for power amplifiers, large loudspeaker cabinets, guitars, electronic gadgets, and other associated equipment. Schools that use these items should plan space and cabinets for their storage as carefully as they do for traditional band and orchestra instruments.

Percussion Cabinet

All small percussion equipment should be assembled in one place for safe storage and accessibility. The percussion cabinet should be equipped with rubber casters so that it can be moved easily around the rehearsal room. Two of the casters should have wheel locks to keep the stand from rolling while being used. Handles can be attached for easy lifting. Drop-leaf extensions on either side of the cabinet top are useful. The shelves should be designed to hold various sizes of cymbals, tomtoms, and tambourines. One shelf should be long enough to hold a set of orchestra bells. Attractive units that provide space for convenient storage, can be locked for safety, and are moved easily from rehearsal room to auditorium are available commercially.

Repair Bench

Every instrumental music department should have some provision for cleaning and repairing instruments. An ideal unit includes a sink with running water, a gas unit to provide flame, electrical outlets, a work surface on which repairs conveniently can be made, and drawers and cabinets below for storing tools and supplies. The size of the repair table and the extent of its capabilities will depend on the mechanical interests and aptitudes of the director as well as on the size of the department. Excellent factory-made repair benches with all the required facilities are available from equipment manufacturers.

Portable Shells

Portable acoustical shells frequently are necessary if musical groups are expected to perform in an auditorium with a high stage house, a large field house, or out of doors where no permanent shell exists. The section on acoustics in Chapter 5 discusses the requirements of reflecting shells in detail.

Sufficient weight is necessary if the panels are to reflect low and middle frequencies adequately. The surface should be hard,

Music folio cabinets are available in several different designs.

and panels need to be reasonably large. It is possible to meet these specifications and still maintain portability. Several commercial firms have developed a variety of shells for choral and instrumental groups. They must be counterweighted for safety, and they should be provided with casters for fast adjustability and easy movement to and from storage. Storage space easily is overlooked even when a portable shell is definitely planned. Six units that nest for storage require a space 73 inches wide, 84 inches deep, and 76 inches high. One company has a unit that combines choral risers, acoustical shell, and built-in lighting into one folding system that is both complete and convenient. Portable and mobile stages for outdoor or traveling performances are available, some of which combine stage and shell into a trailer that can be towed behind an automobile. Custom units designed for a department's particular needs can be made to order by leading equipment suppliers.

A portable shell is not intended to take the place of a regular permanent enclosure for music, especially in a proscenium-type auditorium with a high stage house. As stated in Chapter 5, the temptation to omit this essential piece of equipment should be resisted strenuously. However, a portable shell is better than no shell.

Music Folio Cabinets

Music folio cabinets for chorus, concert band, orchestra, or marching band allow students to gather their music as they enter the room and replace it as they leave. Commercially available units come in dimensions to accommodate various folios and may be combined to fit available space in the rehearsal room. Some instrumental directors prefer a music folio cabinet that will hold 3 to 6 folios in each slot to accommodate various subsections in their musical organizations.

Miscellaneous Equipment

Special situations call for other types of equipment. Many elementary school music teachers have special boxes fitted with rubber wheels and handles to carry songbooks, phonograph records, and other equipment to classrooms. Movable coat and hat racks may be useful in some situations. A flag and stand may be required where a rehearsal area also is used as a small auditorium. Classrooms equipped with projection screens should have curtains or blinds to darken the rooms.

Bibliography

This bibliography includes books and articles mentioned in the text. It also gives references that will provide supplementary information on certain topics the reader may wish to pursue in greater depth. More technical details than are found in the text itself, particularly on the subjects of acoustics and sound isolation, may be explored in some of the titles enumerated here. A few of the books contain pertinent information only in certain chapters. These are obvious from their titles. A number of references are included that deal with theatre planning—a subject that is considered outside the scope of this book, but that must be taken into careful consideration in planning and equipping an auditorium to accommodate both musical and theatrical performances.

BOOKS

American Association of School Administrators. *New Forms for Community Education.* Arlington, Virginia: AASA, 1974.

American Association of School Administrators. *Open Space Schools.* Washington: AASA, 1971.

Appleton, Jon H. and Ronald C. Perera. *The Development and Practice of Electronic Music.* Englewood Cliffs, New Jersey: Prentice-Hall, Inc., 1975.

Beranek, Leo L. *Music, Acoustics and Architecture.* New York: John Wiley & Sons, Inc. 1962.

Carpenter, Thomas H. *Televised Music Instruction.* Washington: Music Educators National Conference, 1973.

Council of Educational Facility Planners. *Guide for Planning Educational Facilities.* Columbis, Ohio: CEFP, 1969

Council of Educational Facility Planners. *What Went Wrong?* Columbus, Ohio: CEFP, 1968.

Courtney, Richard. *The Drama Studio.* London: Pitman and Sons, 1963.

Davis, Don. *Acoustical Tests and Measurements.* Indianapolis, Indiana: Howard W. Sams & Co., Inc., 1965.

Doelle, Leslie I. *Acoustics in Architectural Design.* Ottawa, Ontario: Division of Building Research, National Research Council, 1965.

Educational Facilities Laboratories. *Community/School: Sharing the Space and the Action.* New York: EFL, 1973.

Educational Facilities Laboratories. *The Place of the Arts in New Towns.* New York: EFL, 1973.

Fitzroy, Dariel and John Lyon Reid. *Acoustical Environment of School Buildings.* New York: Educational Facilities Laboratories, 1963.

House, Robert W. *Administration in Music Education.* Englewood Cliffs, New Jersey: Prentice-Hall, Inc., 1973.

Illuminating Engineering Society. *Lighting Handbook.* New York: IES, 1952.

Klotman, Robert H. *The School Music Administrator and Supervisor.* Englewood Cliffs, New Jersey: Prentice-Hall, Inc., 1973.

Knudsen, V. O. and C. M. Harris. *Acoustical Designing in Architecture.* New York: John Wiley & Sons, Inc., 1950.

Lonnbury, Warren C. *Theatre Backstage from A to Z.* Seattle and London: University of Washington Press, 1967.

Meske, Eunice Boardman and Carroll Rinehart. *Individualized Instruction in Music.* Reston, Virginia: MENC, 1975.

Music Educators National Conference. *The School Music Program: Description and Standards.* Vienna, Virginia: MENC, 1974.

National Council of State Supervisors of Music. *Guidelines in Music Education: Supportive Requirements.* Washington: Music Educators National Conference, 1972.

Parker, Floyd G. and Max S. Smith. *Planning Community Junior College Facilities.* Continuing Education Service, Michigan State University, East Lansing, Michigan, 1968; and Council of Education Facility Planners, 29 W. Woodruff Street, Columbus, Ohio 43210.

Parker, W. Oren and Harvey K. Smith. *Scene Design and Stage Lighting.* Third edition. New York: Holt, Rinehart and Winston, Inc., 1973.

Peluso, Joseph L. *A Survey of the Status of Theatre in U. S. High Schools.* South Orange, New Jersey: U. S. Department of Health, Education and Welfare, Bureau of Research, 1970.

Rettinger, Michael. *Acoustics: Room Design and Noise Control.* New York: Chemical Publishing Co., 1973.

Robinson, Horace. *Architecture for Educational Theatre.* Eugene: University of Oregon Press, 1971.

Trythall, Gilbert. *Principles and Practices of Electronic Music.* New York: Grosset & Dunlap, 1973.

Yerges, Lyle F. *Sound, Noise, and Vibration Control.* New York: Van Nostrand Reinhold Co., 1969.

ARTICLES

Davis, Don. "Analyzing Loudspeaker Locations for Sound Reinforcement Systems," *Journal of the Audio Engineering Society.* Vol. 17, No. 6. December 1969.

Downs, J. W. "Acoustics for the Solo Performer," *Instrumentalist.* November 1974.

"Equipment for Electronic Music Laboratories," *Music Educators Journal.* Vol. 55, No. 3. November 1968.

Geerdes, Harold P. "Acoustics for the Music Educator," *The School Musician.* March 1974.

Geerdes, Harold P. "Adjustable Acoustics in Music Performance," *Music Educators Journal.* Vol. 61, No. 8. April 1975.

Jaffe, Christopher. "Design Considerations for a DeMountable Concert Enclosure (Symphonic Shell)," *Journal of the Audio Engineering Society.* April 1974.

Johnson, Russell. "Acoustical Design of Multi-Purpose College Auditoriums," *American School and University.* 1962-1963.

Johnson, Russell. "Acoustics for Music Performance," Parts I & II, *Musical America.* February and March 1960.

Klepper, David L. "An Auditorium for Every Use: Can It Be Built?" *Architectural and Engineering News.* May 1961.

Klepper, David L. "Speech Acoustics for the Theatre," *Journal of the Audio Engineering Society.* Vol. 22, No. 1. January/February 1974.

Klepper, David L. "Theatre Sound and Communication Systems," *Theatre Design and Technology.* No. 28. February 1972 (with Harold Burris-Meyer, Russell Johnson, Christopher Jaffe, Richard Thompson, Ranger Farrell, and C. P. Boner).

Marshall, L. Gerald. "Planning/Designing the Low Budget School Auditorium," *Instrumentalist.* August 1974.

MISCELLANEOUS

Acoustical and Insulating Materials Association. *Performance Data on Architectural Acoustical Materials.* Bulletin No. 32. Park Ridge, Illinois, AIMA, 1973.

Acoustical and Insulating Materials Association. *The Use of Architectural Acoustical Materials : Theory and Practice.* Park Ridge, Illinois: AIMA, 1972.

City of New York. *Building Code: Local Law No. 76 of the City of New York* (Effective date December 6, 1968). New York: The City Record, 2213 Municipal Building, New York, New York.

Educational Facilities Laboratories. *Fine Arts Facilities: Past, Present, Future.* New York: EFL College Newsletter. October 1965.

Educational Facilities Laboratories. *The High School Auditorium: Six Designs for Renewal.* New York: EFL, 1967.

Miller, James Hull. *Freestanding Scenery.* Elmhurst, Illinois: Hub Electric Company Bulletin 121, 1966.

Miller, James Hull. *Small Auditoriums with Open Stages.* Elmhurst, Illinois: Hub Electric Company Bulletin 126, 1969.

United States Gypsum Company. *Sound Control Construction.* Chicago, Illinois: USGC, 1972.

Wenger Corporation. *Performing Area Acoustics.* Owatonna, Minnesota, 1971.

List of Illustrations and Figures

List of Illustrations

List of Figures

Index

Acoustical door, 44 (see also Sound lock)
Acoustical requirements
    auditorium, 36
    gymnasium, 48-49
    orchestra pit, 39
    practice room, 16-17
Acoustics, 44-49 (see also Variable acoustics)
Air conditioning, 43
    auditorium, 52
    practice room, 17
Amplification, 59, 65-67
Antenna, 60
Apron, 36
Arena, 27
Audio systems, 59-62, 66-67 (see also Playback systems, Sound systems)
Audiovisual equipment, 64-69
Auditorium, 27-36
    acoustics, 47
    color, 56
    lighting, 55-56
    playback systems, 66-67
Background noise, 43
Balcony, 35, 39, 48
Ballasts, 55, 58
Band instruments, 64
Battens, 37, 50
Booths (see Control rooms)
Box office (see Ticket office)

Brightness ratio, 53-54
Broadcasting, 15, 60
Budgeting
    audiovisual equipment, 64
    divisible auditorium, 35-36
    initial, 4
    sound isolation, 43
    stage equipment, 38-39
Building codes, 5, 14-15, 33, 40-41
Bulletin board, 70
Cabinets (see Storage)
Cafetorium, 9
Caliper, 35-36
Canopy (see Shell)
Carpet, 12-13, 45, 47
Cassette recorder, 66
Ceiling height, 11-12, 14, 47-48
Ceiling reflective surface, 11, 45, 47
Central stage (see Arena)
Chairs, 14-15, 36, 69 (see also Seats)
Chairstands, 69-70
Chalkboard, 14-15, 18, 54, 70
Chamber music (see Recital hall)
Checklists
    basic planning considerations, 9
    common uses of the auditorium, 31
    intercommunication stations, 61
    stage manager's desk, 40
Choral room, 14-15, 26-27

Notes